Stories from Servant Leaders

The Lessons

The Losses

and

The Part Left Out

By

Randy Borders

Cover Photographer:

Stories From Servant Leaders / Randy Borders
ISBN- 978-1-7923-6276-7

Dedication

This book is dedicated to the loving memory of my spiritual father, Bishop Otis Lockett of Evangel Fellowship COGIC in Greensboro, NC. I met you as a young college student who had nothing but zeal and a love for God. You saw more in me than I saw in myself. I will always be grateful for the lessons you taught and the model of godliness you set before us. You were a true apostolic trainer, releasing spiritual sons and daughters all over the world and your own biological sons to carry on your legacy in the Triad area.

After obtaining my degree, I came back to my hometown in May of 1990 with your blessing to plant a church. I had 'No' idea the church was going to *plant* me. Thank you for making me hang in there when I wanted to give up. You told me, "God never ends on a negative. If it ain't looking positive yet, God ain't finished." Because of all you instilled in me; I am determined to finish my course. I am because of you.

Endorsements

I remember being at the Full Gospel Baptist Church Fellowship PROPEL Conference. This is one of the foremost leadership gatherings in our Nation. We were in Baltimore, MD hosted by Bishop Oscar Brown. I was moving around working and decided to sit in a class of a man who I had heard about but I had never had the opportunity to witness his ministry in person. I sat there somewhere between blessed and amazed but overall, I felt a connection. I believe the reason I feel a connection is because he and I share much of the same message and that is to servants. His clarity, compassion and conviction helped me to understand that Bishop Randy Borders is unquestionably one of the greatest teachers of servant leaders in this generation.

He has proven to be a man that listens and obeys the voice of God, and it's evidence is proven in his ministry of servant leadership.

I know while studying this incredible book and applying it's life altering lessons, your level of understanding and the peace that will come with Bishop Borders very unique and enlightening revelation will assist you in becoming a very effective and effective servant.

In this book, Bishop Borders has personally collaborated with some of the most renowned servant leaders to give us complete access to personal stories on the lessons, the losses, and the part left out when serving your leader.

Now more than ever, this book is essential and critical for anyone serving in ministry or leadership and these same principles and apply them to your life.

Bishop Lester Love
The City of Love
New Orleans, Louisiana

Stories of Servant Leaders serves three purposes. The first is an opportunity to experience the lessons learned by those who were either chosen or chose to walk alongside their leaders. Secondly, if you are reading this book, and you have served in this capacity, you will be encouraged to know your stories may not be so different after all. And thirdly, the Servant Leaders who have authored their stories have been given an occasion to share their journey. What an amazing and creative way to connect those individuals who, on various levels, are responsible for the success of those they served.

The power of serving is phenomenon often overlooked by those who have never served. Sometimes it is even criticized and demonized. But after spending 38 years of my life with one who was consistent and faithful in serving church leaders, I have nothing but appreciation for the Servant Leader. I could not write this without thinking of my late husband, the adjutant of all adjutants, Bishop J. Delano Ellis II. He said, "Those who serve make the best leaders." The stories shared here are only proof the time spent in the shadow is not time wasted or lost.

Dr. Sabrina J. Ellis
Senior Pastor
Pentecostal Church of Christ
Cleveland, Ohio

Bishop Randy Borders lives what he teaches. He truly has a servant's heart and exemplifies what the bible says, "to be kind and compassionate". Enjoy his new book filled with great stories of lessons learned by him and others with a heart to serve.

Elder Robin Ware
Chief Executive Officer
TheWareAgency.com
Atlanta, Georgia

Endorsements

Servant leadership is a paradoxical notion for many. To truly carry out this assignment, one must be willing to humbly wash the feet of those who often kick against the prick of the assignment to lead them into their purpose and destiny. It takes a pure heart and strong determination to consistently take up the "towel" of time, sacrifice & patience to be an example of leading in serving. In this book, Bishop Randy Borders moves beyond the rhetorical into the relational. It gives key points of essential practicum from experienced leaders who live daily lives of "tallying up the true cost" to be a servant leader. It's a must read for those interested in Christlike leadership.

Bishop L. Spenser Smith
Lead Pastor
Impact Nation Fellowship Church
Tuscaloosa, Alabama

CONTENTS

Foreword

I am honored to write the foreword for this book, compiled and edited by my friend and brother, Bishop Randy Borders. Anyone who knows Bishop Borders knows this book is his life. He has and is a servant and what is so amazing is He Loves It!!! I am so glad God used him to call the writers to this task. I know it will be a blessing. Someone has observed history is really the stories of men and women, their lives, their journeys, their experiences, and their memories. History is written every day and every person living makes some kind of history. We all know the famous and the infamous. Their names and stories dot the landscape of our lives, as well as previous and successive generations.

Every day history is in the making and every day someone, somewhere is making history. That truth is what makes this book, you now hold, so powerful and so potentially life changing for those who read it. This is a book of history, of events that shaped and molded the persons who testify on these pages. It is their story of how someone not only contributed to their lives but also made a life changing impact on them, as well. In some ways, the title of this book seems oxymoronic. It combines two words, which seem to have absolutely nothing to do with each other. Look at the words, Servant and Leader. The two seem to be in direct contrast, contradiction, and conflict with one another. The problem, if I can be allowed to use that word, in my thinking, is found in what these words mean in the current parlance of the day.

What does one hear when someone says Servant. I speak now as an African American. More often than not, in our culture, the word 'servant' conjures up one of two images, slavery or grandparents, who worked as maids, butlers, chauffeurs, domestics or what we called in my childhood, "days' work". These are painful images. These images, for many of us, have left a negative stain on the idea of servant. In other cultures, those same examples, make the word 'servant' a pejorative. In this space, these individuals are accustomed to being served and anyone who serves is below them or beneath them. I know I am making a broad point, but it is a reality some struggle to deal with. And so, because of this reality, a servant is seen as less than in most cultures.

Now take the word Leader. Here is a word we love, a political leader, a civil rights leader, a business leader, or a religious leader… you get the idea. A leader is someone out front. They are in charge. Now, there is something to aspire to! You see why I said the title of this book seems to be a contradiction in terms? And yet, there is a place where these two words go together perfectly well. It is in the Kingdom of God.

In fact, a Servant Leader is what the Kingdom is all about. Its focal point is a God, a King, who became a servant. It is the heart of "incarnational" theology. In Christ, God became a man and then announces, "the Son of man came not to be served, but to serve". It is upside down. It is contradictory, but it is the Kingdom way and wonders of wonders, it works!!!! That is what this book, you now hold, is all about. It is the power of servant leadership; how it blesses a life, benefits a life, and makes a life better. Indeed, there are some lessons one only learns when one serves.

Here is what I love about this book and I think you will as well. It is a rich blend of persons and personalities. These people come from various places with diverse backgrounds and all have a different story about serving and leading. It is exciting because it illustrates how God uses all kinds of people. In the Kingdom of God, anyone qualifies to be a servant.

These stories are honest. Look at the subtitle, 'Lessons, Losses and The Part Left Out". That right there tells you it is going to be good. Why? Because when the truth is told, serving is not always easy. There is a price and there is pain. This book reveals both.

Finally, these stories of servant leaders tell how they have found joy in serving. It shares how their lives have not been diminished by serving but rather enhanced and enriched. Open this book, walk its pages, read the stories, learn the lessons, and then look for ways you can serve. You will never regret it and in the end, it will be one of the great joys of your life. The eschatology of the Church declares a day is coming when the Redeemed of the Lord will stand before Him. And, as they are received and rewarded, the words we will hear are these, "WELL DONE GOOD AND FAITHFUL SERVANT". It gets no better than that.

-Bishop Timothy J. Clarke
First Church of God
Columbus, Ohio

Introduction

*"Life is a succession of lessons which
must be lived to be understood."*
Helen Keller

After graduating from high school in 1986, I headed for college in Greensboro, NC. I had no idea God not only orchestrated my steps for higher learning, but He also choreographed my becoming a part of a church that would change my life. After being in college a month, I joined Evangel Fellowship Word Ministries, under the leadership of Bishop Otis Lockett. This is where my perspective on servanthood was created and honed.

Bishop Lockett would always tell us, *"The way you feel about God is directly related to how you take care of His bride, the church."* With this in mind, I wanted to see every part of the ministry excel. I always found myself serving. I had a fervent desire to see our ministry winning. I would do whatever I could to help my leaders achieve their goals. In short, I served. We all served. It was all I knew.

At the age of 21, just six days after my graduation The University of North Carolina at Greensboro, I started pastoring. I had not yet been to seminary. I knew little about church-planting or leadership development. I did know how to serve my leadership and the church at large. In fact, it probably was the only thing I was good at. I built my life around serving God's people and leaders in particular. Not only was it my love and passion, but it became my specialized niche. I gave my heart to it. For years, it was my primary focus. I developed a burden to see leaders encouraged, strengthened, and supported. I wanted to be to others what I so often needed myself.

Samuel Chand, the leadership guru, says, *"Those who faithfully support from the bottom are often unseen. That doesn't diminish their importance or the need for them."* There is so much done in the office, on the teams, and for the vision by those who do not get credit for it. Though the extent of their impact may not be known, it is their contributions we celebrate when vision comes together.

I wrote my first book on Adjutancy and second-tier leadership in 2005; my second book on Adjutancy I wrote in 2018. And I wrote 'More Than A Mentor' in 2017. From 2005 to 2018, I traveled the country extensively I taught leadership support, helps ministries, and servanthood. I did every kind of service to lift leadership including, but not limited to conferences, staff trainings, pastoral celebrations, leadership installations, etc. These assignments often required transparency, sharing the weight, burdens, and functions of servant leaders. These ministry assignments forged bonds and connections with servant leaders that would remain for years.

During this process, I was startled to find every adjutant, armorbearer, assistant, CEO, CFO, department-head, and second tier leader had *stories.* These *stories* or testimonies were literally a part of their spiritual formation and servant-leader development. It is our stories that shape us. What made their service in ministry so powerful was their journey. There were stories of sincere sacrifices; ventures of faith; misalignment with superiors; seasons of rebellion; blatant betrayal; triumph over trials; and bounce back from failures. Yet, they all helped them find God in a fresh way and in time gave them a profound depth of character. My concern was I taught principles and textbook lessons but was unable to highlight people; specific individuals who had walked servant leadership out.

Those who serve, often fail to realize how they are affected by what they do and how what they do affects others. Though they serve with the aid and assistance of the Holy Spirit, they cannot divorce what they have experienced (whether good or bad) from who they are. Who they have come to be as a servant leader is an accumulation of their leadership experiences and how they were handled. We often want to romanticize our roles, making them void of the human element. But our roles come with an incredible emotional, psychological, and physical impact. Yes, we are God's people; but we are still *people,* nonetheless. Every exchange and every interaction are lessons whether comprehended or not.

Many lessons learned were not in a scripture text. There were untold stories of losses due to or in spite of their unwavering commitment to serve the vision of the local church. Lastly, there were elements to their assignment that caught them unaware, things 'No' one could have ever prepared them for. This I call, "The Part Left Out". Thus, the subtitle of the book, *"The Lessons, The Losses, and The Part Left Out"*. I spent over a decade teaching principles of servant leadership. I found people believed the principles of leadership and servant-hood; but they failed to find scenarios with which they could identify.

For years, I heard stories individuals thought were unique to them. Yet, the more I talked to other servant leaders, the more I realized we all have so much in common. My questions then became, "Who does for the servant leader what they do for others?" If they make things go well for others, who ensures they are well? If they are gifted to make ministry look easy, who helps them when "easy" is really "difficult"? I learned certain things are germane to all of us who lead from the second seat. Thus, I reached out to some of those who I have personally watched assist key leaders in making vision reality. The purpose of this book is to combine multiple stories of servant leaders in one place as a message of encouragement and strength for those who serve. Their documented experiences make this book full of "living" lessons.

-Bishop Randy Borders

PART ONE:

THE LESSONS

1

The Power of Focus

Elder Robert D. Maxwell
Director of Communications | Elizabeth Baptist Church
Atlanta, Georgia

In February 2017, I was presented with an amazing opportunity to come alongside Dr. Craig L. Oliver, Sr., as the Director of Communications for Elizabeth Baptist Church and his personal assistant. I was excited about the opportunity to do something new. Six months earlier, I sensed a shift in my ministerial trajectory, but I had no idea how it would manifest. Through a series of what can only be described as providentially orchestrated events, I was being positioned for what was a God-ordained transition.

Given this transition originated in the mind of God, one might conclude it should be relatively easy; but that is only partially true. The contextual backdrop of my transition was enmeshed with expectations from outsiders, perceived disloyalty, and an overall misconception of the purpose and providence of God - - all from persons OUTSIDE of the relationships involved. In other words, there was a discordant symphony of outside voices weighing in on a situation requiring a God-breathed, **focused** response. This **focused** response was critical in order for me to walk in tandem with God's purpose for my life.

Focus is defined as: **directed attention; adjustment for distinct vision; and a state or condition permitting clear perception or understanding**. On this transitional journey, I was about to learn a valuable lesson about the inherent power of focus. If I was going to successfully matriculate through the lessons God was teaching me via this transition, it was going to take **focused** alignment with His Word.

A Rich Ministerial Legacy

I am a proud descendant of the Morton Family ministerial dynasty. My maternal grandfather was Bishop C.L. Morton Sr., a powerful preacher of the Gospel and a humanitarian trailblazer. In addition to his philanthropic work to advance the cause of human rights, he founded 11 churches in Canada and the United States of America. He also hosted radio programs in Chatham and Windsor, Ontario, reaching millions of listeners on both sides of the border. He was the progenitor responsible for the births of the nine powerful children, including Bishop C.L. Morton, Jr.; Bishop James Morton; Bishop Paul S. Morton, Sr.; and my mother, Evangelist Nancy Morton Maxwell.

The Winds of Change

Although my ministerial life was advancing quite nicely at my uncle's church, I began to sense the shifting winds of change. I did not quite know what it was, but there was a hunger for something different within me. To be abundantly clear, there were absolutely no problems at all, for me, at my uncle's church. My kids were born and raised there and my wife, a minister in her own right, was progressing as well. I repeat, there were no issues at all. Yet, I could sense God shifting me – which of course caused me some concern.

I had always looked at my assignment at my uncle's church as just that…an assignment. We were not there because of the familial connection, but because God had providentially placed us there. One of the challenges you encounter when you are related to the pastor is navigating the course of your individual call. People, because of your connection to the pastor, tend to view everything you do through the lenses of your familial relation. Admittedly, there were times when I felt even my uncle viewed what I was doing in the church through the optics of our family connection.

I do not say this in a disparaging manner, but as a family we adhere to a certain level of excellence. And yes, in alignment with that ethic of excellence, family is held to a higher standard. Though I felt the winds of change blowing in my life, I was not actively looking to change anything concerning my church engagement. However, God in his infinite wisdom had begun to orchestrate my transition before I even realized it.

I was doing some freelance work for Tehillah Magazine and was asked by the Editor-in-Chief to interview Dr. Craig L. Oliver, Sr., concerning his upcoming PROPEL 2016 Conference. I initially declined the opportunity. The Editor-in-Chief, Lyn Sanders, was a good friend and insisted I do it. Her exact words to me were, "He speaks the way you write, and I think it would be a great connection." Reluctantly, I agreed to do the interview.

It was a great interview and I left thoroughly impressed with his position as a pastor and a leader with great insight. His office would later contact me, through Lyn's recommendation, for additional writing projects and over the course of the next few months we would engage on that level. It was not until the end of the year when Dr. Oliver presented me with the possibility of joining the staff of Elizabeth Baptist Church, I really connected what I had been sensing in my spirit to what was happening in my experience.

I was both ecstatic and reticent at the same time. On the one hand, there is nothing like sensing the Hand of God on a move you had been discerning all along. I like challenges, so the notion of going somewhere where I was not the pastor's nephew and could viewed solely as an individual, was very appealing. On the other hand, I was discreet and hesitant because I did not want my uncle to believe this had anything to do with dissatisfaction with the church or him as a pastor. Many members feel this way when negotiating moving their membership to another church. For family members of a pastor in this position, this feeling of anxiety can be magnified exponentially.

Ultimately, I followed the leading of the Lord and made the decision to accept employment at Elizabeth Baptist Church, as well as transition my membership. Ironically, membership at EBC was not a condition of my employment. Dr. Oliver made it abundantly clear I could still maintain my membership at Changing a Generation. He was sensitive to the fact I belonged to my uncle's church and did not want to cause any issues in that regard. I, however, recognized this transition would require me to move my membership as well, and I stated my intention to both Dr. Oliver and Bishop Morton.

Both men of God gave me their blessings on this move, for which I am grateful. Interestingly enough, the pressure, opposition, and subsequent lesson on the power of focus, did not come from any of us directly involved, but from spectators looking in from the outside. Once the transition was made public, I began to get an earful from friends, supposed spiritual sons and daughters of my uncle's, and even random people who had heard of my pending transition.

The first lesson I learned about the power of focus, was the power of focused alignment. Though the transition was a positive thing happening in my life, I was not without uncertainty, fear, and a level of discomfort concerning my move. If you are not careful, outside voices, not in alignment with what God has spoken over you, can wreak havoc on your ability to carry out what God has directed.

LESSON #1: Focused Alignment
PSALM 1:1-3

[1]Blessed is the man that walketh not in the counsel of the ungodly, nor standeth in the way of sinners, nor sitteth in the seat of the scornful.[2]But his delight is in the law of the Lord; and in his law doth he meditate day and night.[3]And he shall be like a tree planted by the rivers of water, that bringeth forth fruit in his season; his leaf also shall not wither; and whatsoever he doeth shall prosper.

KJV

By definition, the word alignment means to exist in accord with something or someone. It denotes agreement with another or to walk in step with another. Alignment indicates walking in congruence. A picture of Godly alignment is depicted the above-mentioned text. Believed to be written by King David, the great Psalmist, Psalm 1 outlines the blessedness and power connected to walking in agreement with the counsel of the Law of the Lord. It stands in contrast to the utter destruction associated with walking misaligned with the purposes of God, and by default walking in the counsel of the ungodly.

How Could You Do This?

Perhaps one of the most perplexing phenomena in church culture to me is when spiritual sons and daughters overstep their roles and begin to infringe upon the biological family dynamics of their perceived spiritual parent(s). When it was initially released I was leaving my uncle's church to go to EBC, I received so much unsolicited "advise" from people who felt legitimately offended by my decision. For them, it seemed I was betraying my uncle and his ministry.

I cannot underscore this enough. From day one, I had my uncle's full support and blessing. In fact, he made it a point to identify, for Dr. Oliver, my ministerial gift and to make sure it was going to be utilized. The two of them had come together to ensure my overall success in ministry. This sense of betrayal was coming from men and women outside of our family and ministry circle who felt it necessary to speak, though not directly involved.

In all honesty, a small part of me was concerned my uncle might perceive my transition as a betrayal. While we do not often have conversations regarding church/family relationships from this dynamic, there is a sense of obligation felt when you work in ministry with family. This obligation rests in the comfort pastors feel knowing you are looking out for their best interests. Moreover, in a culture where sometimes people are looking to advance, you as a family member, are simply there because you love them. Transition, in this space, can often feel like a brutal interruption in an otherwise smooth operation.

One day while vacillating back and forth on this very issue, the Lord brought to my mind Psalm 1, *"Blessed is the man that walketh not in the counsel of the ungodly nor standeth in the way of sinners, nor sitteth in the seat of the scornful."* As I meditated on this particular passage, I recognized I had not aligned myself with ungodly counsel. This transitional directive came from God Himself to me. This was not a product of my own mind, but it was a directive from God. How could I NOT do this? That became my response when asked how I could do such a thing! I intentionally and deliberately focused on aligning with what God directed to drown out the noise of the naysayers. People are people, and they are certainly entitled to their opinions. I determined however; I would not spend an inordinate amount of time justifying my movements to people when I knew I was aligned with what God had directed.

LESSON #2: Focused Confession
He Had Plans for You!

In the 2nd Verse of Psalm 1, the psalmist declares, *"But his delight is in the law of the Lord, and in his law doth he meditates day and night."* In other words, it is the blessed man who rightly aligns himself with the purposes and plans of God revealed in His Word. It is the blessed man who has learned to walk in focused agreement with God! This focused agreement hinges upon deliberately confessing what God has said.

A ministerial colleague at my uncle's church, who also happened to be a dear brother and friend, helped to underscore the value of focused confession in my life. One night while attending the Morton Brothers Revival held at my Uncle James' church, the subject of my impending transition came up. He could not understand how or why I would be leaving CAG, where we had come up together in ministry. He made a statement I will never forget. Unlike the others who were on the outside, he was definitely an insider. I realized there was nothing malicious about his intent. He said to me, "Robert, you cannot leave, because Bishop had plans for you." My immediate response to him was, "But what about God's plans for me?"

As Pastor of New Members, my wife and I had very visible roles at Changing a Generation. We were both active in ministry; and I am certain there were those who saw us remaining in leadership at CAG, alongside my uncle. For many, it seemed ministerial suicide to leave a place, where I was already established in ministry and related to the pastor, for a place where I was an unknown. Moreover, there were unfounded conversations regarding whether or not my uncle would name me as a successor upon his retirement. For some, my leaving felt like I was abandoning my family heritage, as well as any ministerial advantage I had.

When my buddy reminded me of the plans everybody else had for me, I redirected him to what really mattered, which were God's plans for me. I confidently reminded my friend "the steps of a good man are ordered by God". Everything I spoke thereafter agreed with the steps God had given to me for this transition. I did not have all of the details, but I did not need all of them as long as I was assured God had spoken to me. I was very intentional about watching the words I confessed concerning my transition. My declaration, my words, were focused specifically on aligning with what God had spoken and being in harmony with His will. This intentional direction in my confession would program my mind to align with God's direction and subsequently my actions would as well.

I will never forget one day I was preparing for a period of fasting. I told myself I wanted God's guidance and direction, but honestly on an unconscious level, I had an outcome I wanted to happen. In my mind, fasting was supposed to bend God's will toward what I wanted. As I was fasting, I remember the Holy Spirit speaking to my heart so clearly saying, "This fast is to get you aligned and in agreement with MY purposes not to manipulate me into doing what you want." I was so shocked! Almost immediately, the confirming scripture of Proverbs 19:21 resonated in my spirit, *"Many are the plans in a person's heart, but it is the Lord's purpose that prevails."*

Focused confession of God's Word is key to, not only shutting out the voices of the naysayers, but rightly aligning our hearts with His will. It was not enough for me to simply think on what He had spoken to me. I had to focus my words, so they were in alignment with what He had directed me to do. The fruit of focused confession in my life was a mind fully persuaded regarding God's intention for my life.

LESSON #3: Focused Movement

In the 3rd verse of Psalm 1, the psalmist declares, *"And he shall be like a tree planted by the rivers of water, that bringeth forth fruit in his season; his leaf also shall not wither; and whatsoever he doeth shall prosper."* In other words, the person who is strategically focused on the counsel of God moves as an indomitable force. This person, by way of their alignment with God, can withstand opposition, is productive at the right time, preserved from destruction, and successful in all of their endeavors. Have you ever tried running or driving against the wind? When the wind is against you, we call it a headwind. A headwind is defined as wind blowing from directly in front, opposing forward motion.

Moving against a headwind requires an excessive use of energy. When you are trying to make progress against the force of a headwind, you have to exert power greater than the wind to overcome its opposition. People use more energy, vehicles use more gas, and it can make for a bumpy ride, all when moving against a headwind. The aforementioned headwind scenario is akin to what it is like not to walk in focused alignment with God. It requires more energy! You are working hard and going nowhere. You are using time and resources to go somewhere God has not sanctioned. You are wasting your grace trying to make things happen God has not ordered or ordained!

Focused alignment with the will of God strategically places the wind of God's favor at our backs and allows us to move forward with the aid of His Grace.

Whereas doing things on our own was akin to trying to move against a headwind; alignment with the will of God is analogous to moving with the assistance of a powerful tailwind. With the wind now congruent with your direction, progress is easier, and you do not have to exert as much effort to advance. My alignment with the purpose and plan of God placed the wind of His favor at my back and made for a smooth transition. I am a firm believer when you do it God's way and focus on His directives, He guides the process from start to finish. It would have been easy to allow my attention to be diverted to the other conversations, but because I was aligned in my heart and my confession was focused; I was determined in my actual movement.

The same people who were vocal about why my move was the wrong one, were able to bear witness to God's Hand upon me in a new framework. I have had more ministerial opportunities in my new context than in any prior setting. Moreover, my positioning at Elizabeth Baptist Church was the perfect place to combine my operational expertise with my ministerial gift, which was the best of both worlds for me. It was never my desire to prove anyone wrong. Those wishes would tend to come from selfish motives, and God does not honor self-promotion.

The same focus guiding me through acceptance of my imminent transition, strategically moved me forward into what God had planned for me. All to, and for His glory. In all God does, He does it well. There is a great power in focus, but great power is predicated on what you choose to be your focal point. Focusing on the Word of God and His voice will ensure you walk out God's intent for your life. That in and of itself is the power of focus.

Elder Robert Dion Maxwell was born and raised in Detroit, Michigan to the union of Elder William Maxwell and Evangelist Nancy Morton-Maxwell. Elder Maxwell was born into a God-fearing Christian home. He accepted the Lord Jesus Christ into his heart at the tender age of six years old. He was an active member of the Mount Zion Church of God in Christ where he learned the virtues of holiness and offering a life sacrificed to God.

In pursuit of excellence Elder Maxwell sought out a diversified educational experience to maximize his God-given potential. He earned his Bachelor of Arts Degree in Psychology in 1997 from Oral Roberts University and his Master of Business Administration from Keller Graduate School in 2002.

Robert was licensed to preach the Gospel and later ordained as an elder of the church under the leadership of Bishop Paul S. Morton, Sr. while serving faithfully at Changing a Generation Full Gospel Baptist Church in Atlanta, Georgia. Vocationally, he currently serves as the Director of Communications at Elizabeth Baptist Church under the leadership of Dr. Craig L. Oliver, Sr. He also serves as the personal assistant to Dr. Oliver as well as a member of the Collaborative Preaching Team of Elizabeth Baptist Church. Elder Maxwell and his wife Sherita are the proud parents of two children, Jaden Robert Maxwell, and Sydney Elise Maxwell.

REFLECTION

The Power of Focus

"Recognize what is worth your focus. Trim the fat and finish strong."

One thing I have learned through the years is for every move you make in ministry and in life, there will always be distractions. Sometimes those distractions are circumstances and sometimes they are people. Both must be treated with the same regard if you are going to reach your goal. A wise man once said, "My focus is to remain focused." Here are a few tips to help.

- Put people in their proper place in your life. Because you have a history together does not automatically mean you have a future together. Choose wisely who you take forward.

- When it comes time to make major shifts in ministry, have a personal conversation with your pastor for the sake of clarity. Do not let them hear the move you are contemplating from gossip in the local church. That gives way too much speculation and misunderstanding.

- Know that faith-moves are just that… faith moves. They may not be understood by all, but they should be respected. There were times when as a pastor, I did not think the timing was right for a particular leader to transition from their ministry post. Even though I was not quite on board with their decision, I owed them my support (even in their risk) because their faithfulness and dedication in service to the ministry.

- Do not be so focused on your new assignment you do not stop and appreciate those who helped you and groomed you to the place you currently are. Never allow people to pit you against your pastoral leadership during your transition. It is important to show appreciation for opportunities you have been extended in the past.

- Never underestimate the power of your pastor's blessing. God honors it.

- Alignment with God and purpose will cause the floodgates of favor to open on your behalf.

2

Serving as a Son

Shawn R. Mason II +
Senior Pastor | The Freedom Church International
General Secretary | St. Mark Holy Church of
America, Inc. New York, New York

*"And it came to pass, as they still went on, and talked,
that, behold, there appeared a chariot of fire, and horses
of fire, and parted them both asunder; and Elijah went
up by a whirlwind into heaven. And Elisha saw it, and
he cried, My father, my father, the chariot of Israel, and
the horsemen thereof. And he saw him 'No' more: and
he took hold of his own clothes and rent them in two
pieces. He took the mantle of Elijah that fell from
him…"* 2 Kings 2:11-13a

I am a firm believer God sends people into your
life for a reason. The reason is not always clear initially,
but as time goes on the scales begin to fall from our eyes.
Timing also plays a role in understanding of one's place
in your life, including the time they enter, the time they
exit the time spent in between. The relationship between
the prophets Elijah and Elisha has always intrigued me.
From Elisha's introduction to Elijah, all the way to their
earthly separation, it was a journey worthy of
observation.

In their initial meeting "the son" was marked by
"the father". It is there the son has to make a destiny
decision. He leaves his home, family, and inheritance to
follow a complete stranger. Elijah's boldness to place
the mantle on Elisha is matched by Elisha's boldness to
follow Elijah. Fathers must lead, sons must follow.

There is a debate on how the relationship happens. Does a son choose his father? Does the father choose the son? Can spiritual paternity be undone?

The concept of "Spiritual Father" and a "Spiritual Son" is quite interesting to say the least. I must preface this literary contribution by stating the word "son" is not exclusive to the male gender in this context. If I may be completely honest, being a "spiritual son" is no easy task both in life and death. Many of us are still attempting to quantify this subjective topic. It really depends on who you ask. Our definitions of things are usually contingent on what lenses we are looking through.

I am, what some may call in the 21st century, a "ministerial statistical anomaly". Currently, I serve as the Senior Pastor of The Freedom Church located in Brooklyn, NY. Prior to planting Freedom with my wife Lady Niakeeya, I attended and served at my home church for over 30 years. Keep in mind "attending" is not the same as "serving". You can be a ministry bench warmer for decades never fully plugged into the vision and mission of the house. I have been blessed to sit under the same leadership throughout my entire life. Even in leaving *(we will get into that a little later)* I remained submitted to my Bishop until his passing, while still serving our reformation and his successor. I understand every "son" has a story, and no one's journey is the same. However, I still feel like my story and insight can be a blessing to many.

One of the challenges of sonship begins with trying to identify *"when did this happen?"* I was a member from birth and grew up at my home church. My parents both belonged there. My paternal and maternal grandparents, as well as my great grandparents were all connected to the ministry in some way. My Father in God, the Late Bishop Nathaniel Townsley, Jr. was always THERE. It is still difficult to come to grips with the reality of his absence. There are times where I want to send him a text message and then I am forced into the unpleasant truth. And, to try to piece the story together is more difficult than I initially thought. It almost seems more appropriate to start at the end.

Bishop Townsley passed away on April 5, 2020 at a time where the world was experiencing the height of the Coronavirus pandemic. Prior to his passing, New York City had already seen a number of surprising deaths from ministry leaders. My late Father in God was a man of vision, foresight, and great wisdom. He was in the hospital for an extended period of time for a heart condition and was preparing for his earthly departure. One of his last words referring to me *was "When I go, Shawn will know what to do."* Hearing those words from his successor, after learning of his passing, felt like a tremendous weight placed on my shoulders.

I prided myself on being obedient, loyal, and unwavering. But now, having to serve and fulfill the instructions of my late father placed me in a precarious position. I had coordinated countless funerals for prelates and Christian leaders of all ranks and varying levels of influence. To attempt to do justice for my own beloved Father in God, in the height of a pandemic amidst an unprecedented death toll amongst Christian leaders, was an arduous task.

"Shawn will know what to do" rang in my ears and as much as it was seen as an honor, it was equally a burden. The reality was, for the first time in over 35 years, one of the most consistent figures in my life was gone. Upon hearing of his passing, I pretended like I was okay until the phone call ended. I hit the floor like a ton of bricks and sobbed uncontrollably. All I remember hearing was my 6-year-old son asking, *"What's wrong with Daddy?"* All I could think, **"SHAWN DID NOT KNOW WHAT TO DO!"** The man who christened

me, baptized me, married my wife and I, licensed me, ordained me, and installed me was gone. You have to understand something. I was never really into sports, the arts, etc. Church was "my thing" and my Bishop was like Michael Jordan to me. I am still to this very day trying to sort out *"Where do I go from here?"* My dedication to the **MISSION** was now poised to be questioned seeing the **MAN** was no longer on the scene. What kept me level was my dedication to the **MESSAGE** he taught me.

Several things pose a challenge to serving as a son. One of the greatest challenges I experienced as a spiritual son was having to balance my natural family and my church family. I was blessed to grow up in a two-parent household with my Mom and Dad. Although, my Dad grew up in church and was ordained as a Deacon, he was not attending regularly for some time. I was selected to be an Adjutant at the age of 14 years old. I was excited and humbled to serve. I took my job very seriously. I was called upon to serve the man who was like Superman to me.

I'm an 80's baby and when I was growing up, my Bishop had these really thick sideburns. In my attempt to look like the Man of God, I would take strips of my biological father's electrical tape and put it on the sides of my face while I was pretending to be him. Most church babies simply played "church", but me…I played "Holy Convocation", complete with processionals, vestments, communion, ordination and of course, preaching.

At times, there was a strain in the relationship with my natural father. For several years, he battled with substance abuse. Yet, before he closed his eyes in death 2010, he was sober and had rededicated his life to the Lord. During the course of his addiction battle, church became my saving grace. Working, serving, and traveling with the church was a way of escape for me. At home, there was vocal resentment toward the church, because I was genuinely more comfortable there than I was at home.

I can remember my father was upset because I wanted to go to church when we had a mandated "family night". In a fit of anger, he roared, "BISHOP IS 'NO'T YOUR FATHER, I AM YOUR FATHER!" However, it was difficult for me to digest this from a man who had ceased to be emotionally available; who was there but was not present. Bishop filled a void for me, he understood me, and he was genuinely concerned about my well-being. He paid $80 an hour for weekly 2-hour math tutoring sessions because I was struggling in math during my senior year in high school. So, the whole "Bishop is not your father" thing really did not register for me.

Prior to my natural father passing away, he and I were able to rebuild our relationship and start the process of sorting some things out. I honestly praise God for that opportunity. It really made me think how blurred the lines can really become when you hopscotch from the natural to the spiritual. Through churches, we build familial relationships. We become "uncles & aunties", "play cousins", and "godparents". We end up vacationing together, aka "going to convention" and we spend a great deal of time together. We sometimes are guilty of building a life in a bubble; excluding those who do not fit the mold or just do not understand. In some cases, we become closer to each other than blood relatives.

Jesus said to Phillip, "He who has seen me, has seen the Father." (John 14:9) Now, do not judge me but it was a joke between Bishop Townsley and I. I would be tasked with serving as his emissary, liaison or representative. He would ask at times "Do I have to go?" or "How was it?" My response would often be, "When you see the son, you've seen the father." That was the burden of sonship; being a visible reminder of where you come from. I have been blessed to travel the country and meet some outstanding people. Few places have I gone where I did not hear the words "How is Bishop doing?" Honestly speaking, I never grew tired of hearing that. I come from good stock and am proud of my heritage.

Yet, being intricately connected to the one you have been called to serve has its benefits, burdens, challenges, and pressures. "Serving as a Son" took on an entirely new light for me as I really began to put some things into perspective. I began to make the stark contrast between natural paternity and spiritual paternity. Most times the lines get blurred, roles get confused and sometimes positions get unclear.

I have come to realize over the years to be a natural born son, you really do not have to do anything other than just "BE". Although you may have the pressure of living up to your last name or you may have to deal with the unreasonable expectations of those who wish you were more like your father, ultimately your sonship will never be challenged. You can be a "bad son", a "disappointing son", or even a "prodigal son". Either way, you are still a son. This is not the case with spiritual sons. Our legitimacy is tied to our acts of service, public deference to our spiritual fathers and most importantly our perceived loyalty. Allowing any of those elements to slip for one reason or another can turn your ministry life into a daytime talk show where they question "ARE YOU THE FATHER?"

"Son" is a label or a title which carries with it a great weight. A title in this context is defined as *an appellation of dignity, honor, distinction, or preeminence attached to a person or family by virtue of rank, office, precedent, privilege, attainment, or lands"* as stated in Merriam-Webster's Dictionary. Titles are absolutely necessary in matters of protocol, as to denote rank and to maintain a healthy acknowledgement of authority.

Patti Digh wrote, *"Don't say you're a writer if you're not writing. Even if you are writing, don't call yourself a writer. Say instead, 'I write.' It's the verb that's important, not the noun."* We cannot allow ourselves to be confined by labels. You are much more than you appear to be. Your actions announce who you truly are, not just the title in front of your name. I often fought with this in my life as a spiritual son. For those who are spiritual sons, it is different. We cannot "just be", we must "do". But even in 'doing', there is still a blessing. Bishop Townsley would often say "being is the seed of doing." In other words, you cannot effectively DO what you are NOT. This shows a direct link between our actions and our identity. As a spiritual son, the two are undeniably connected and must be held in the forefront of our minds.

I often say *"pressure does one of two things. It will either burst a pipe or it will make a diamond. You are ultimately in control of what you allow your pressure to do for you."* Sonship is not without its pressures, including the pressures to succeed (particularly when your father is of some renown). It is so interesting to me; my Bishop was a musical genius. He was a singer, songwriter, composer, and the list goes on and on. My home church was known for its musical ability. With no exaggeration, there was a time where about 75% of the church could really sing. Unfortunately, I did not inherit that portion of the mantle. It was always funny to me. I would walk into churches and they would lead me to the organ. I would be utterly confused. Their response would be "You're from Bishop Townsley's church, I assumed you played".

There is another pressure, which is to remain consistent. As a good son, you should always be in your place. As a son, all I have ever wanted to do was serve and serve well. The pressure came in for me when I began to grow, develop, and widen my skillsets. It was then I was being called upon to preach, serve, or coordinate matters of protocol for other churches and leaders. The pressure in this for me was to remain loyal and consistent. Not that my heart was not at home, but like every other budding young cleric you want to explore and gain experience.

Bishop Townsley was a man who afforded me so many opportunities. I was able to join him on a Musical Tour of Italy when I was 17 years old. Now remember, I said I did not inherit the musical part from him. My willingness to serve even from an early age afforded me such an amazing opportunity. He gave me opportunities to preach regularly on Sunday mornings, to teach Bible Study on Tuesday nights and to even preach in his stead periodically.

What I appreciated about him was he still allowed me to serve outside of the house. Of course, there were instances where he would not give me the go ahead. And because it was seldom, I did not murmur or complain (at least out loud). The real pressure was not allowing outside opportunity to determine my loyalty. Prospects may be tempting, and opportunities may be lucrative. Sometimes, it will almost be so good you can convince yourself this is the will of God concerning your life. However, I was blessed to have a great spiritual father. I did not view my staying put as staying stuck. Your ability to stay stationary for an extended season does not equate to being stuck.

Added pressure comes from people who have "spiritual daddy issues", those who allow their ambition to override the purpose of God for their life, and from those who are disgruntled with leadership. I learned how to deal with the pressure by trying to keep my eyes on the big picture. I figured out my blessing was tied to my staying close. I did not stay close to receive a blessing, but I received the blessing because I stayed close. I am aware everyone has a different journey. Some people are assigned to people for certain periods of time. Our assignments to each other lasted for almost 36 years.

Additionally, the pressure of trying to maintain your personal life while doing the work of the ministry can be extremely difficult. If we are honest, when you are in ministry there is no such thing as a "personal life". We often battle with trying to keep the worst parts of us a secret. Therein lies the source of the pressure. In all actuality, our lives in the church and outside of the church are closely intertwined. Bishop L. Spenser Smith wrote a song called "Surgery", one of the lines says, "a public success, but a private failure." I can attest to that during the course of my life.

Success does not always equate to popularity or trans-regional influence. Any amount of success in a field or an area is still success. I was what some may call "the golden child". I must say I vehemently disagree with this notion, although some of my church family would beg to differ. It would often be said *"Shawn can do no wrong in Bishop's eyes."* However, there were some dark times in my life where my personal indiscretions were not pleasing in the sight of God and also cast a stain on my Bishop.

The challenge of being a church kid, an aspiring preacher, and one who genuinely loved God became a lot. There were times where I have failed miserably on this Christian journey. When your leader endorses, validates, and affirms you publicly, everything you do becomes a part of their brand, institution, and even legacy. Our lapses in judgment, moral failures, or actions unbecoming of our leaders can easily cast a proverbial blemish on our fathers. Those who questioned your ascension will look at your leader with the "I told you so" face. Those who have looked up to you may either feel the pattern of behavior is acceptable or may be so discouraged, it turns them away from ministry.

The pressure of representing my leader while still representing myself proved to be a lot for me. I was in college and had a baby on the way. The timing could not have been worse. I had been serving as an Adjutant for a few years. I was preaching here and there; but not formally licensed. My first thought upon learning I had a baby on the way, was not *"How am I going to handle being a young Dad?"*. It was not *"Oh man, I have disappointed my family."* My initial thought was **"BISHOP IS GOING TO KILL ME!"** Though he was not that type of man, but I held him in such high esteem.

What he thought of me mattered. Bishop Townsley corrected me, loved me, covered me, and never ceased to affirm my calling. In a bold move, he licensed me shortly after my now almost 15-year-old daughter was born. If it were left up to some circles, I would have been silenced until the rapture or publicly shamed and deemed disqualified.

In any relationship, you will be challenged. My most memorable challenge during my time of serving my father was having the "BIG TALK". For those who have been called to pastoral ministry, you know about this conversation. I was zealous, excited, and hopeful. I had been trying to work up the nerve to come to my father and say, "I feel led to plant a church". It took me about 3 years to have the initial conversation. I was scared out of my wits! I will never forget, I asked him on a Sunday can I meet with him that week. Because he and I spent a great deal of time together, I always had the opportunity to speak with him personally. He looked at me with a confused but pleasant look and said "Sure, son". This conversation would change the climate of our relationship in ways I do not think I was prepared for.

How do you tell "the voice of God for you" when you have heard from God on your own? He and I met on a Tuesday and I timidly said, "I feel led to plant a church." Bishop looked at me and filled his cheeks with air and then said, "I knew this conversation was coming. So, when are you thinking about planting?" It seemed good to me; I gave him my timeline which was radically different from what he was comfortable with.

Over the next two years or so, he and I would have a series of "intense fellowships" as I called them. In my eyes, what may have been viewed as the departure of a son was really the expansion of a father. Bishop Townsley was a nurturer who wanted to keep those under his charge safe. In one of our conversations, he said "You have the gift of focus. You are able to lock in on something, but you lack peripheral vision at times. As a shepherd, you have to do both." At first, I was greatly offended. I thought I was doing pretty well. Everything was all planned out.

In 2017, he gave me his blessing to plant The Freedom Church. After much prayer, discussion, and soul searching, he formally released me to do what God called me to do. The challenge in serving as a son is sometimes God will give you an assignment which may differ from what everyone else has become accustomed. I was at the crossroads of do I stay, or do I follow purpose. I was released. Yet even in release, I was and still am a son. The benefit of being a son for me is a having a traceable lineage. I know where I come from, I know who birthed me in ministry and I know to whose legacy I am perpetually attached.

Sonship is not easy, and as I matriculate in ministry, I am seeing being a father is not easy either.

With my natural father, there were some things I did not understand until I had a wife and children of my own. It is the same thing with Bishop Townsley. Some things did not make sense to me until I established a work. I will forever cherish the memory and endeavor to preserve the legacy of my late Father in God, Bishop Nathaniel Townsley, Jr.

Shawn R. Mason II is a servant, thinker, and visionary leader. A Brooklyn native, he serves as the proud Senior Pastor of The Freedom Church which officially launched in September 2017. He was reared from birth in the Historic St. Mark Holy Church under the leadership of the late Bishop Nathaniel Townsley, Jr. serving in several ministry capacities. It was there he was licensed to preached and ordained to the presbytery. Presently, he serves as an Overseer and General Secretary within the St. Mark Churches. He studied at the University at Albany, where he pursued a Bachelor of Arts degree in History. He also received a Bachelor of Theology from Dominion Theological Seminary. Presently, he is enrolled in a Master of Divinity program at North Carolina Theological Seminary.

A much sought-after lecturer and episcopal protocol consultant, he is the visionary and lead facilitator of the "Empowering Servants Symposium" an in-depth and informative series of workshops for those in the ministry of helps. For 20 years, Shawn has had the privilege of serving in the adjutancy. For over a decade he has served Adjutant General for a multitude Episcopal Consecrations and Ordinations and is currently working on his own manual for ministers of protocol.

Overseer Mason's greatest joy is doing life with his wife, Lady Niakeeya Mason and being the father of four outstanding children.

REFLECTION

Serving As A Son
"Sons might outgrow their father's public achievements, but never their private counsel."

I Kings 19:19-21 *"19 So Elijah went and found Elisha son of Shaphat plowing a field. There were twelve teams of oxen in the field, and Elisha was plowing with the twelfth team. Elijah went over to him and threw his cloak across his shoulders and then walked away. 20 Elisha left the oxen standing there, ran after Elijah, and said to him, "First let me go and kiss my father and mother good-bye, and then I will go with you!" Elijah replied, "Go on back, but think about what I have done to you."*

When Elijah met Elisha, Elijah was looking for his successor; but Elisha had no clue. The senior leader just put his cloak/mantle on him and told him to think about what just happened. The young Elisha was at his father's house plowing. He recognized his next level was in Elijah and left all familiar to follow him. He thought about the weight of the coat laid on him he could not possibly wear, but the senior leader saw what he could become. I really like the fact Elijah waited until Elisha went back and honored his parents. He did not just snatch him away and disregard his present authority. From that day Elisha served Elijah as a son. Upon the rapture of Elijah in a Chariot of fire, Elisha looked up and cried out to him in the most endearing term, "MY FATHER, MY FATHER."

- The word "father" is synonymous with "responsibility". Ask yourself the question, "Who holds you accountable for walking in your God-given assignment.

- SONS owe their existence to a FATHER. Someone gave them a chance, and opportunity, or a platform. No matter how long ago it was, find a way to say "Thank You" again.

- It is never right to be a recipient of your leader's influence and platform, while simultaneously despising their wisdom and correction.

- Your spiritual father has something you do not have because they know something you do not know. BE TEACHABLE.

3

Resisting Familiarity

Derrick Noble
Lead of the Office of Special Projects |
Mount Zion Baptist Church
Chief of Staff to the office of Presiding Bishop |
Full Gospel Baptist Church Fellowship
Nashville, Tennessee.

I was serving as the Executive Administrator to Bishop Clarence E. McClendon, Pastor of Church of the Harvest in Los Angeles. My leadership role was clarified at the beginning, and healthy boundaries were established. But over time, I became like a member of the McClendon family. I was given access to spaces where I participated in gatherings and sat at tables as a brother and a friend. I welcomed the opportunity to have a close relationship with a family revered by many people around the world.

Many times, the settings were extremely casual, and I shared a bond with members of the McClendon family I had longed for with my own family. This was a journey some could only hope to embark upon. Many doors were opened to me. I had incredible successes as a direct result of my association with Bishop McClendon, and I was extremely grateful for the opportunity to serve alongside him and members of his family.

But at some point, I had to be reminded I was an employee of the ministry and not a family member. Once, we were having dinner with Pastor Benny Hinn, and Bishop McClendon shared his thoughts about moving his mother to California. Rather impulsively, I said, "Man, that's great! This will allow her to be closer to you and her grandchildren." Both men looked at me and smiled. At first, I thought this meant they agreed with me and approved of my input. But that was not the case.

As soon as dinner was over, with a quickness, Bishop McClendon rebuked me for speaking so casually. He reminded me of the importance of respecting my employer and, more important, of respecting God's chosen vessels. I was stung by Bishop McClendon's correction. However, like a great leader, he was also quick to show love, reminding me I should be prayerful and led by the Holy Spirit in how to conduct myself, especially in front of the team members I had the responsibility of leading, ensuring the vision happened.

That experience was sobering for me. Though I had been included in many family discussions, it was not appropriate for me to speak into family matters, especially in that setting. I had presumed a familiarity I should not have assumed. I had to be reminded I was hired to serve in the ministry and to render service to the people of God.

Bishop McClendon also taught me it is rare for leaders to find people they can trust and with whom they are comfortable sharing their personal and ministerial vulnerabilities. It is rare because leaders need people who are able to discern the appropriate settings and know how to communicate accordingly. I had failed to properly discern the setting and allowed my familiarity to lead me away from my assigned role.

In that moment, I began to understand how important it is to have a trusted working relationship with generals in the Lord's church and how familiarity can damage the relationship. Having started in a corporate setting, I realized the importance of establishing healthy boundaries with coworkers. It was important to do the same in this environment, as well. I thought I could let my guard down when I started working in the ministry. After all, the Bible says we are all connected like brothers and sisters as God's offspring; and sibling relationships are usually close, intimate, and without pretense. And while that is true, the church is still a place of business. Relationships need to be respectful, and leadership should always be revered.

I grew up in church, so I am no stranger to being around internationally known leaders. And although my proximity to great leaders at an early age served me well, perhaps it also gave me a false sense of familiarity when I worked closely with them as an adult. My father, Fred Matt 'Noble, was a Baptist preacher; and my mother, Herley Mae 'Noble, was a licensed minister in the Pentecostal Church. Growing up, I attended Greater Bethany Apostolic Church, pastored by Bishop Robert W. McMurray.

It is now City of Refuge and is pastored by Bishop 'Noel Jones. As a family, we were faithful members of Greater Bethany. My parents were leaders there and exposed me to church life up close and personal. I was privy to many things going on behind the scenes the average person in the pew never knows. It was quite natural for me to befriend pastors, ministers, visiting clergy, other church leaders, and their families. These close relationships have always been part of my life; and, later, they informed how I envisioned my own journey into full-time ministry as an adult.

Over the years, I heard the preaching and teaching of some of the greatest pastors and evangelists in the world. I was influenced by diverse leaders such as Bishop Iona Locke, Bishop Carolyn Showell, and Bishop T. D. Jakes. Their leadership development training was the springboard for my interest in ministry and my being equipped to serve God's people. But I had yet to learn how familiarity with leaders can be a double-edged sword.

Familiarity, in the context of ministry, connotes sharing a close acquaintance or relationship with a leader. This type of relationship is often marked by informality and a lack of restraint because few boundaries exist between the leader and the person working alongside. Similar to family members, persons involved in such a relationship usually have personal and intimate knowledge of each other.

They feel free to confide in each other sharing vulnerabilities they would never reveal to mere associates or strangers. As humans, we are social beings. So, it is normal for us—even leaders—to want to bond with like-minded people and avoid loneliness, something the greatest leaders in ministry struggle with. Unfortunately, I did not understand the pitfalls I might encounter, with familiarity, at the beginning of my ministry journey.

I met Bishop Joseph W. Walker III in 1998, and almost immediately, we recognized we were kindred spirits. So, when he asked me to leave Los Angeles and move to Nashville to serve alongside him in the ministry, I did not hesitate to join him in service. Over the years, our relationship has grown. The more we have gotten to know each other, the easier it has become to be close friends and colleagues in the gospel. In fact, calling each other "bro," "dude," or "man" became normal and acceptable.

Bishop Walker writes in his book *'No Opportunity Wasted'*, "Relationships over rules—one of the most important lessons I've learned when embracing opportunity and managing vision is that I have to put relationships over rules. Rules are necessary in order to maintain order and structure, however, never become so legalistic with your vision that you are not willing to compromise for the sake of a relationship. By no means does this suggest doing things that are illegal or unethical. What I am suggesting is that you develop an ethos within your organization where rules don't prevent needs from being met."[1]

When I first met Bishop Walker; I had not developed discernment; nor learned all I needed to have effective relationships with leaders. I had not matured enough to handle the type of working relationship forming between us, and it was easy to cross the necessary boundaries established as protective mechanisms. There were times when I was asked to serve and assist in particular areas of the ministry, but because of 'familiarity', I thought those assignments were beneath me. As a result, I delegated them to others.

One time, I traveled out of town with Bishop Walker to a speaking engagement. I was extremely exhausted from a long work week. I was also managing personal emotions brought on by my unwillingness to accept my parents were aging and ill. Yet duty called, and it was time to serve my leader in a different capacity. I was glad I had accompanied Bishop Walker on the trip. I wanted to receive a word from the Lord without being called away during the service to handle a business matter.

We entered the sanctuary when the worship experience was high. I joined in as soon as we were escorted to our seats. It was a powerful setting. I lifted my hands in worship, and I sang and cried out to the Lord. I found myself getting lost in the experience, and nothing else mattered to me other than being refreshed in the Holy Ghost. We had traveled hundreds of miles to get to this engagement, and I was spiritually, emotionally, and physically worn down. I had been focusing on family matters and needed a breakthrough.

As soon as I was engulfed in the Lord's presence, Bishop Walker tried to hand me his Bible to hold until it was time for him to minister. I thought to myself, *Man, don't you see me engaged and engulfed in this worship experience? Don't you see me with this ugly cry expression on my face? You need to hold your own Bible while I receive from the Lord!* We looked at each other in silence, and then he handed his Bible to one of the armor-bearers from the host church.

I thought, *Dude, first of all, I am your chief of staff, and this assignment should be given to someone else. Second, you know me well enough to know when I am lost in worship. I am not thinking about you or anyone else because my spirit needs to be ministered to. Third, you have two hands just like I do, and you can hold your own Bible.*

Soon the service shifted, and protocol was established. An overwhelming feeling of sadness came over me. The Holy Spirit reminded me of my assignment to serve, and I remembered an important lesson Bishop Walker had shared during a leadership training:

> "One of the most important lessons any leader will ever learn is that of serving. I am where I am today because I learned how to serve before God made me a steward over anything. I view it not as a chore but a wonderful opportunity for growth and development. So many want to be served and believe they can bypass the work of ministry and serving and experience elevation. This is a sad truth. "Serving is essential to leadership."[2]

This was my ah-ha moment. I had just taken advantage of the relationship with my leader, and I had disrespected him through my familiarity with him. I had crossed the boundaries. It was inevitable. I had allowed myself to think more of myself than I ought. This fact was a sobering moment for me, and I was saddened. Even with my years of experience, I had not matured enough to find a balance between relationship and service.

It is unfortunate when leaders find trusted persons they consider friends, only to discover they are not mature enough to know when to differentiate between relationship and service. I believe it is possible to maintain a respectful relationship between the leader and team members. A certain level of maturity and discernment is necessary for all parties to know what role to play and when to step into which role at the appropriate time.

However, too often, we become friends with our leaders, or we have been the leader and befriended our team members. In these moments, we lose a sense of service in the relationship when the boundaries are crossed. But why do we try to navigate these tricky waters when we have seen the fallout time and time again? One reason is leaders, like most everyone else, experience loneliness. And it is difficult for them to find like-minded people they can trust and confide in without worrying their vulnerabilities will be exposed for the world to see.

I noticed a pattern with people who serve in leadership roles. They have a strong handle on things in the workplace, intuitively knowing when it is the right time to launch new initiatives and to share expected outcomes because they are both big and small thinkers. This comes naturally to a successful leader. Yet with many successes, most leaders find themselves extremely lonely. I have served in various leadership roles for the past four decades in the corporate and religious sectors.

At times, leadership can feel like riding a roller coaster. There are feelings of joy in having the influence on the future and the history of an organization, and there are also feelings of loneliness because, as a leader, you are set apart.

In the beginning of my journey in leadership, I experienced a loneliness that was almost crippling. I was shocked by how lonely it could be. My perception of leadership was wrong because I assumed, as a leader, I would always feel empowered and on top of the mountain, experiencing wins with very few losses. That is not how it works. As a leader, my list of friends in the workplace decreased at an exponential rate. Things changed drastically, and I realized it was because I was no longer a friend, others felt they could confide in. I was now the leader—the person who set the rules, told people what to do, and was not fun to be around, which made leadership lonely.

At first, I resented not having friends at work and experiencing success as a result of healthy working relationships fostered by collaboration and teamwork. But I realized some people do not know how to separate the roles, and performance can suffer. Turning off the friend-mode is not always easy. Friend mode makes it hard to lead, coach, and hold team members accountable. As I matured as a leader, I came to realize leaders are chosen for their ability to lead; challenging others to be more than they ever imagined they could be, not to be friends with those they are leading.

I have not completely mastered turning off the friend-mode in the workplace. I am learning how to define relationships in such a way my role as a leader is clear and respected because of my experience and what I can offer the team. Many leaders do not know how to set that bar, and too often they fall into the trap of befriending their team members. Why? Because they are lonely and, like most people, want to be liked, accepted, and heard. It is not impossible for leaders to be friends with team members. However, the roles have to be clearly delineated in order to gain the respect necessary to drive performance levels to the height of success.

So, I understand why leaders are intentional about forming relationships with trusted people. And I have also learned serving alongside a leader is not for the faint of heart. At times, I am involved in intense conversations, making it difficult to foster a sense of collaboration with those who have not embraced the vision of the leader. A good leader should know the heart of the senior leader and be able to represent him or her in the same spirit.

The relationship between the two should be similar to the relationship between Moses and Aaron, who worked together closely as leaders in ministry serving God's people. For those of us who are familiar with the biblical story of Moses and Aaron, we learned God allows us to be positioned in places and situations best suited for us. I received the honor of being referred to as an Aaron early in my working relationship with Bishop Walker. He tells leaders much of his success is a result of hiring to his weakness. Choosing capable people to work together allows him to accomplish much more than he could do alone.

It is important to be prayerful when choosing a person to be in the number two position. When the right person is chosen, he or she can represent the leader in such a way they compensate for the weaknesses, vulnerabilities, and feelings of inadequacy of the senior leader. Pastor Chuck Swindoll gives a beautiful account of the relationship between Moses and Aaron in his book, *Great Days With the Great Lives*:

> [God said,] "Aaron, go to Moses' side now. He's on a long, wilderness road, heading for Egypt. Your younger brother has been through some tough things. He needs a soul brother, right now. . . ." Do you have a friend with whom you can face the realities of your life? You may have lots of friendships in your life, but you'll probably never have more than a couple of friends on that deeper, spiritual, soul-to-soul level. You can tell such a friend anything that God is doing in your life, and you'll find a warm reception and deep affirmation. If you don't have such a friendship, tell God about your longing. He's the same God who moved Aaron's heart down in Egypt while Moses was walking alone on the desert road. And remember, the best way to find such a friend is to be such a friend.[3]

Aaron was chosen to serve alongside Moses, and he was eventually anointed. But we learn from Scripture he became impatient and disobedient, as we all do as human beings. He began thinking more highly of himself and asked his sister, Miriam, "Has the LORD indeed spoken only through Moses? Has he not spoken through us also?" (Numbers 12:1-2). Because they were siblings, perhaps the familiarity Aaron and Miriam had with Moses caused them not to respect him as God's chosen vessel to lead the people. When I read this passage, I often wonder if Aaron had become too familiar with Moses during his time of service.

There have been times when Bishop Walker has shared intimate details of matters dear to his heart, making me feel more like a brother than an employee.

As a matter of fact, he has called me family and included me in family discussions and gatherings. Building relationships and collaborating with trusted team members is extremely important. It has been an honor and a privilege to be considered family by a leader who is revered by so many. For almost two decades, we have cried, laughed, and grown together while serving God's people.

At Mt. Zion, I lead the Department of Special Projects. This area encompasses the Office of the Presiding Bishop for the Full Gospel Baptist Church Fellowship International, where I serve as the chief of staff to our presider, Bishop Walker. As the chief of staff to the presiding bishop, I am responsible for the organizational readiness of new projects and vision implementation. Much of my responsibility is focused on understanding the various components after vision-casting sessions, collaborating with key stake-holders and team members to execute the vision, and identifying and confirming available resources. But there are many others that require my attention.

Leaders often rely on me to offer advice and permission to engage others or to complete assignments. Organizational readiness requires I maintain a healthy working relationship with those I lead and serve. My relationship with the visionary requires a strong partnership with the senior pastor and presiding prelate, and my role must complement him well. Bishop Walker encourages leaders: "[to not] delay your destiny by attempting to do everything by yourself. You need the right people in your life to ensure you are able to make great things happen. If you are going to be successful, you have to make the right connections. This begins by surrounding yourself with people who are dedicated to their vocation."[4]

I have been given wonderful opportunities to serve with awesome leaders. I once served as a senior public health administrative analyst. During the initial interview, I felt a connection almost immediately with my soon-to-be boss. She was agnostic but was intrigued by my work experience in the religious industry. After the two-hour interview, she invited me to lunch with her and her husband. Our conversation switched from formal interview questions to more personal questions about my upbringing in church and my time in volunteer and paid leadership roles. She and her husband were interested in my journey, and they took the time to get to know me better.

Despite their leadership successes, they experienced loneliness. They had no children and had lost their parents and siblings, so they were quite alone in the world and had become guarded in developing relationships outside of their marriage. But once they had the opportunity to know more about me, they welcomed me into a close friendship that developed over the years. We spent holidays together, and the couple also sought peace and a purpose-filled life by attending special services I invited them to, after which they stopped questioning the existence of God. Over the years, we learned how to serve together, to respect one another's differences, and to gain knowledge from one another, all while not becoming too familiar. And I am glad to say we are still friends today.

I have learned many lessons over the years, and many of them were painful. I had to face the truth about myself. I is easy to form friendships with people in the workplace because that is where you spend most of your time. "In the workplace, for example, employees will spend roughly half their waking hours working and living in the environment you create [with] the leader."[5] But boundaries are easily crossed, and it becomes difficult to establish and respect healthy boundaries. It is hard to avoid personal conversations, but some topics just are not appropriate for leaders and team members to share. Everyone must recognize and value their place and be willing to contribute to the whole while not becoming too familiar, which can cause leaders and team members to lose focus and not be able to fulfill their assignments.

It takes time to develop a good working relationship with a leader. According to writers James Kouzes and Barry Posner, "Leadership is a relationship between those who aspire to lead and those who choose to follow. Sometimes that relationship is one-to-one. Sometimes it is one-to-many. Regardless of the number, in order to thrive . . . leaders must master the dynamics of the leadership relationship. Leaders have an important contribution to make to our understanding of the dynamics of the leadership relationship."[6] I have learned it is not impossible to have a friendly, family-type relationship with a leader. However, it takes work and effort not to become too familiar and to disrespect the one God has assigned you to serve. It's important to have someone in your life you respect and allow to keep you in check of your motives and your attitude.

Bishop Randy Borders is one of those people in my life. I revere him and thank God he said yes to cover me and my family. Bishop Borders encourages us to "get in the habit of showing your God-given spiritual leader the utmost respect. Make a lifestyle choice to honor your spiritual parents just as fully as God wants you to honor your earthly parents."[7]

This fact does not mean the leader you are assigned to automatically becomes your spiritual parent, but you should honor him or her as though they are in that position. Build the connection with a sense of reverence and with the confidence you have been chosen to serve in this assignment at this moment in time.

There is no substitution for the time it takes to build confidence, trust, and loyalty. But in doing so, it is important to deal with the struggle of being a friend to your leader. It is the tension of not becoming too familiar while grasping the importance of facilitating your assignments via the leader's vision.

---

[1] *'No' Opportunity Wasted: The Art of Execution*, by Joseph W. Walker III (Heritage Publishing, 2017); page 99.

[2] *Leadershifts: Mastering Transitions in Leadership & Life*, by Joseph W. Walker III (Abingdon Press, 2014); pages 72-73.

[3] *Great Days with the Great Lives: Profiles in Character*, by Charles R. Swindoll (Thomas Nelson Inc., 2007); page 74.

[4] *'No' Opportunity Wasted*; page 46.

[5] *The Servant: A Simple Story About the True Essence of Leadership*, by James C. Hunter (Crown Business, 2012); pages 26-27.

[6] *Christian Reflections on the Leadership Challenge*, by James M. Kouzes and Barry Z. Posner (Jossey-Bass, 2004); page 119.

[7] *More Than a Mentor: Understanding and Growing in Your Relationship With Your Spiritual Father*, by Randy Borders (Sermon to Book, 2018); page 53.

DERRICK NOBLE

Derrick D. Noble, Organizational Strategist, is a native of Santa Monica, California. He provides oversight to the Office of Special Projects at the historical Mount Zion Baptist Church of Nashville, Tennessee. One of the current projects includes the New Level Community Development Center. With over 25 years' experience in Project Management, Derrick also serves as Chief of Staff to the Presiding Bishop (Bishop Walker) of the Full Gospel Baptist Church Fellowship, International.

Upon graduating from Trevecca Nazarene University with honors, he received his Bachelor of Arts in Organizational Leadership & Management and is continuing his educational journey. Derrick's record of success and extensive involvement in non-profit sectors, public health, human resource management, and leadership development has made him a catalyst among his peers. One of his most notable accomplishments to date is his work with Dyan Cannon, Hollywood actress, director, producer, and editor. As a part of his commitment to community involvement, Derrick has served the Riverside and San Bernardino' counties in the areas of Public Health, Inland Empire HIV/AIDS Planning Council, and Grants Management.

He married Sherelle Noble, in 2010 and together they have a son, Derrick Jr. They reside in Nashville, TN.

REFLECTION

Resisting Familiarity

"Your vision is too important to keep subjecting it to the sabotage of fake friends."

When you spend a lot of time investing your life in the vision of a leader, it is highly possible to become too familiar and common with them. Leaders have to always be kept in awe to the people. Once "awe" is gone, respect is the next thing to go. You do not have to be formal at all times, but you cannot allow your informality to lead to disrespect. Your pastor must be respected and held in high regard.

- In Genesis 37, Joseph's brothers were never blessed by him as long as they could identify him. It was not until time and distance passed and they could not recognize him; then they were able to see him in a position to assist them.

- Moses' sister Miriam got too familiar with him and only recognized him as her brother, but not her God-given leader. She started talking about her pastors' wife and God smote her with leprosy. (Numbers 12)

- You would think it would be ok to laugh at your husband, but God did not find it funny when David's wife laughed at him dancing unto God in front of all of Israel. God shut up her womb. Be careful how you criticize the decisions of God's anointed. You do not want to find yourself criticizing what God's hand is on. (2 Samuel 6)

4

The Principle of Honor

Dennis R. Hebert, Jr.
Senior Pastor | Beacon Light Baptist Church
Hammond, LA

There are certain Kingdom principles we are introduced to through proper education in the Word and then there are others which come through both experience and education. Honor is such a principle. Certainly, the scriptures are replete and crystal clear in instructing and commanding believers to embrace honor as a Kingdom key. Yet, the full revelation of honor is gleaned through the opportunities we have to walk out these principles in a real-life context.

When I was in college, I began as a biology major with aspirations of being a medical doctor. Immediately, upon beginning my undergraduate course work, I was made aware there are two aspects of the biology curriculum: the lecture and the lab. I can remember it like it was yesterday; the lectures were on Monday, Wednesday, Friday, and the lab was on Thursday. What was taught in the lecture needed to be practiced in the lab. The two went together to prepare the student for a practical understanding of coursework.

It was not until I began serving my pastor I realized this same rubric was in play in ministry. Everything taught in lecture would be tested in the lab. What made this a critical revelation in biology and in ministry is lessons ignored in lecture can prove tragic in the lab. God never tests what he has not first taught, so it is extremely important for servants to pay attention during the lecture. Although the leader's responsibility may cause them to be present for multiple services and hear their leader teach several times a week, again remember this principle. God never tests what He has not first taught. The kingdom of God operates on this key principle and success in serving in ministry is obtained by paying attention in the lecture so you can pass the lab.

I gleaned this revelation as I was serving my pastor, Bishop Darryl S. Brister. He is a man who not only teaches honor, but consistently practices the principles of honor in serving his spiritual father, Bishop Paul S. Morton. When I connected with Beacon Light Baptist Church under Bishop Brister's leadership, I could sense the strong culture of honor prevalent throughout the ministry. It was a kingdom principle taught by Bishop Brister and echoed by those in leadership. It was there I learned honor is more than lip service, public esteem, and respect. I came to understand honor and serving the man of God deals with assisting in carrying the burden of ministry. More importantly, true honor is measured by one's ability to receive the rebuke of the leader and remain unwavering in loyalty, dedication, and consistency.

I recall during my early days of ministry. As the New Members' Pastor, my life had so much going on at that time. At 23 years old, I was attending seminary three nights a week. I had just married my college sweetheart and my career with a leading pharmaceutical company was showing tremendous promise for promotion. I was so excited about serving my pastor's vision, my church; and the amazing opportunity to work on the ministry team with some amazing people.

What I did not anticipate was the self-serving politics and gamesmanship that accompanied serving on a ministry team. Suffice to say in any ministry context, the human factors of misaligned motives accompanied with insecurity and jealousy will always be present. I began to realize in order to remain loyal to my leader, I had to endure those who were around my leader. I would have to withstand the attitudes and animosity of those who felt I was inexperienced or unqualified to hold such an office. Not to mention there were several individuals who felt entitled because of their senior status; and were unhappy this unknown youngster was promoted.

I heard countless sermons on remaining faithful to the call of ministry, while dealing with detractors and those who would discourage and disappoint you. But this was now my lab. This was the test of honor. Would I honor the assignment given to me by my leader despite those who did not approve or support his decision?

Imagine for a moment the psychological pressure. I was young with options and opportunities. My friends, who were not a part of my church, would tell me I was crazy for enduring all I had going on in my life. It was so much easier to say enough and resign from this volunteer position, focusing my efforts on career, family and enjoying the life God had afforded me. I did not know it then, but my loyalty to the assignment my leader had given me was being tested.

I was being asked to honor people and protocols working for my demise. I felt like David when he was assigned to remain loyal to Saul despite the constant attacks against him. The lesson learned was if we only honor the honorable then we have no reward. The enemy always tests your honor towards your leader because it is a covenant connection. If the devil can get you to sow dishonor towards your leader, he can disconnect you from the anointing flowing from the leader into your life.

There was a time, Sunday night communion services were quite popular. These services are a tradition that has all but faded away in our modern culture. However, once upon a time, churches would have Sunday night services once a month to observe Holy Communion. This was a big deal for our church and the highlight worship service of the month. An aspect of the Sunday Night communion services was the right hand of fellowship. All of the new members who had joined the past month would be formally welcomed into their new church community.

The new members would be invited down to the front of the pulpit where all the Elders and leaders of the church would extend a handshake and welcome them before the entire congregation. It was the responsibility of the New Members team to ensure these individuals were present and on time to participate in this aspect of the service. I think you can see where this story is going.

One Sunday night, we announced over 100 individuals had joined our church that month. Bishop Brister stood and asked for those 100 individuals to come down and receive the right hand of fellowship. To my utter embarrassment, only 15 individuals responded. There were at least 1000 people in attendance that night and I felt like all 2000 eyeballs were staring in my direction at this dismal response.

To add insult to injury, after the right hand of fellowship was over and the music ministry was singing, Bishop Brister walked over to me (with all the haters and distractors watching) and shared his disappointment with the low turnout of our new members. Although this took place almost 20 years ago I still remember the stern words he spoke to me that night, "You are a better leader than what was shown tonight."

I do not think I remembered anything else taking place in the service to say the least. In talking with my team after church, several admitted they did not contact the new partners as they should to ensure their attendance for the right hand of fellowship. I went home and told my wife, this is the last straw, I quit. not only did I have to deal with political shenanigans from the team, Now I had to endure a public rebuke for something my team of failed to do. Nope! I am done with this. I do not need this in my life. I quit. He did not have to handle me like that in front of everyone.

The next morning the Holy Spirit reminded me honor is not about what happens when we agree, but honor is a lifestyle. If one is too big to be rebuked then one is too small to serve. It was days after I realized just as a natural father rebukes his children so to must spiritual fathers. I realized honoring fathers is more about your role assisting in what God has called them to do and remaining faithful to your assignment.

In Genesis 22, Abraham took the wood and laid it upon his son Isaac. As an honorable son, Isaac carried the wood up the mountain. Sons honor their fathers/leaders by helping the father/leader carry the wood. The burden and pressure of the assignment is to be shared by sons and daughters who honorably and faithfully serve their leader. When I share in the burden of ministry, I am displaying my honor. Honor is more than lip service. Honor is long suffering. Honor is going when we do not fully understand what God is doing in the life of the leader.

DENNIS HEBERT

Dennis R. Hebert, Jr. was born in Los Angeles, California on 'November 30, 1977 to Reverend and Mrs. Dennis R. Hebert, Sr. He was reared in Baton Rouge, Louisiana and later relocated to New Orleans, Louisiana where he married Tranecia Williams and is the proud father of three sons Dennis III., Dylan, and Drake Hebert. He attended Nicholls State University in Thibodaux, LA and is a graduate of the University of Louisiana at Monroe (1999).

Elder Hebert's commitment and passion for the word of God motivated him to pursue his theological training at the Darryl S. Brister Bible College and Theological Seminary in New Orleans, Louisiana where he studied Pastoral Studies. Dennis received his Master of Divinity at United Theological Seminary, Dayton, Ohio in December 2015. On December 18, 2005 Pastor Dennis R. Hebert Jr. was installed as the Senior Pastor of the Beacon Light Baptist Church of Hammond, with approximately 1800 members and two campuses.

Bishop Hebert holds a personal passion for ministering the gospel to men. He has taught at various men's conferences around the country and has authored two books, entitled *"The Champion's Mentality: A Blueprint for Kingdom Manhood" and "The Champion's Mentality: Daily Devotional –Daily Instructions for the Kingdom Man."*

REFLECTION

The Principle of Honor

"If they do not honor you, a healthy relationship cannot exist. Adjust your expectations. It will save you a lot of pain."

Mark 6:1-6 *¹ Jesus left there and went to his hometown, accompanied by his disciples. ² When the Sabbath came, he began to teach in the synagogue, and many who heard him were amazed. "Where did this man get these things?" they asked. "What's this wisdom that has been given him? What are these remarkable miracles he is performing? ³ Isn't this the carpenter? Isn't this Mary's son and the brother of James, Joseph, Judas, and Simon? Aren't his sisters here with us?" And they took offense at him.⁴ Jesus said to them, "A prophet is not without honor except in his own town, among his relatives and in his own home." ⁵ He could not do any miracles there, except lay his hands on a few sick people and heal them. ⁶ He was amazed at their lack of faith.*

Honor means to hold someone in high-regard and respect. Honor in ministry is a game-changer. Even in the ministry of Jesus, He could not do any miracles because there was no honor. They knew he and his family well, so they honored him as a carpenter; but not as a miracle work-er. Where there is honor and confidence; phenomenal things can be accomplished. But there is such a thing as an "honor-killer". It is hard to honor someone who lacks in-tegrity. Just as leadership integrity always attracts honor. The lack of leadership credibility will breed dishonor. You can get the respect of people when you deal in truth and equity.

- You cannot expect honor if you are not honorable. It is easy to celebrate the gifted and humble; but it is difficult to celebrate the gifted and arrogant.

- If you do not know how to give honor you will never receive honor. You reap what you sow. (Galatians 6:7)

- Thirty times in the scriptures the word "honor" is connected to money or gift-giving. It is not enough to honor with lip service. If someone pours into your life and helps you live better; you should not think it robbery to sow back into them. (I Corinthians 9:11)

- Elders who rule well are considered worthy of double honor.(I Timothy 5:17) All Judah brought Jehoshaphat presents and they were called honor. (II Chronicles 17:11)

5

DO IT DIFFERENT

Pastor Joshua C. Chiles
Senior Pastor | The Life Center
Abbeville, SC

November 15, 2017 is a day I will never forget. It was the day the baton was passed to me in ministry. Some may ask what does the "passing of the baton" mean? Various dictionaries describe it as handing over a particular duty or responsibility. When I was passed the baton and installed as the Senior Pastor, I was given the duty and responsibility to lead and oversee the position, the people, the purpose, and the promise of The LIFE Center in Abbeville, South Carolina.

The phrase "passing the baton" is an athletic phrase that comes from the sport of track and field. It takes place during a relay race. In order to finish the race, a baton has to be successfully passed three times, leaving the "last leg" enough room to either to take the lead or compete in a way to catch up. An important part of passing the baton is the one passing it still has to keep running, yet being mindful of the passing zone, until the receiver is successfully moving forward. There is no other place in the Bible describing the relay race we run as Christians better than 2 Timothy 4:7, *"I have fought the good fight, I have finished the race, I have kept the faith."* As believers we are all a part of a relay race designed to have a finish line.

My mother and father have pastored for over 30 years. My entire life has revolved around what many would call "church." I have seen the passing down of many ministries, the transitions of many pastors, and the passing of many batons. It ails me to say the majority have not gone well. Passing a baton during a relay race, must be done delicately yet strategically. The same attention must be shown in ministry. As a former athlete, I have seen many relay teams lose because they fumbled the handoff. I have seen just as many races lost because the team dropped the baton which results in automatic disqualification. The fumbling and dropping of the handoff can cause a team to lose an entire race or a ministry to lose its entire vision. Just like in a race, every moment counts in ministry.

Four examples in Scripture stand out when talking about the passing of the baton. First and foremost is our greatest example, our Lord and Savior Jesus Christ passed the baton to His disciples. Second, the Apostle Paul, the tent maker from Tarsus who passed it to Timothy. Third, the prophetic Priest Elijah passed it to Elisha. Lastly is where we will later lay out an anchor; with a devoted friend of God, Moses who passed it to Joshua. This passing must always be spirit led, but there is a sequence that cannot be ignored. A sequence many missed but could not afford to. This sequence of timing, technique and communication is of great significance and is found best in the first chapter of Joshua.

In the first chapter of Joshua, we see Joshua receiving the baton from a deceased Moses. He has been serving for forty years and now it is his time. He has engaged forty years of learning and listening in order to lead. To lead effectively takes time. And never forget there is a specific time for you to take your rightful place in ministry. You never want to be installed prematurely. I honor and credit my leaders for not responding to their time, but honoring God's time to put me in position. Now I have pastored, and I understand the necessity of the wait. Of course, at that time I thought was being held back. I had a gift. I thought I was ready, but a gift does not prepare you to lead; character and self-leadership does.

Leadership is not only a role. It is a responsibility. One of the major roles is the ability and the assignment to influence. I am not talking about achieving the ambitious feat of influencing your congregation, though that is a part. I am speaking of the feat of influencing you. When the baton is passed, it is vital to know who you are. You must know so you cannot only lead the people but also lead you.

In every ministry, there is a person who needs to be influenced. The number one person is you. You cannot influence a flock if you cannot influence yourself. Joshua became one of the most accomplished and influential leaders in the Old Testament. I believe his ability to lead himself played a key role in his success.

Joshua 24:15 is the focus scripture for my entire family and my personal ministry. In this text, Joshua voices a level of leadership not many have the courage to voice. Joshua states *"But if serving the LORD seems undesirable to you, then choose for yourselves this day whom you will serve, whether the gods your ancestors served beyond the Euphrates, or the gods of the Amorites, in whose land you are living. But as for me and my household, we will serve the LORD."* That is the New International version (NIV).

The Joshua Chiles Version (JCV) says, "Y'all can do what you want, serve who you want but as for me and my crew we're rolling with God." To me, this is real leadership. Joshua, son of Nun, could proclaim these things because he understood three powerful keys. These are three keys Joshua Chiles had to learn. Learning them have since turned my losses into lessons.

Lesson #1 UNDERSTAND WHAT IS DEAD.

In the first chapter of Joshua, the first thing the Lord says to Joshua was "Moses my servant is dead". This is information Joshua would have already known. Joshua was Moses' personal assistant. Everywhere Moses went, Joshua was there. So surely, he knew when Moses transitioned. The question must be asked is "Why would God tell Joshua something he already knew?" Well, I am glad you asked. God, in this text, was reiterating the fact Moses was dead. He has no intention of raising him up. When you receive the baton, there are some things that must die and stay dead. There are some things you as a leader must move past and there is no time to grieve.

God told Joshua "Moses is dead and it's time to cross over the Jordan." I had to learn I will never be able to cross over into what God promised if I am always tied and tethered to what God allowed to die. It is going to be hard to lead and be emotionally tied to the past. Moses had this issue. He was constantly grieved by the people. God was letting Joshua know he could not be tied and tethered to his emotions, while believing he could lead this congregation into greatness.

Early in my pastorate, I became overwhelmed emotionally because of dealings with the people. There must be a separation from the leaders and people. My leaders will be the first to tell you they struggled in this area. It is impossible to be available to all the needs of all the people all the time. This is something they attempted to do much like Moses. Thank God for the Jethro Principle (Exodus 18).

As a transitional leader you must be focused enough to see what does and does not work. You must be able to discern what needs to live and what needs to die. Now, this gets complicated when you have taken the baton but the leader who passed is still holding on. My advice to any leader holding on to what they passed, let go and see where your next place is. My advice to those who are receiving the baton but do not feel their leader has let go; let go and find the place you can lead effectively. Have the conversation. Talk through the concerns, but most importantly, seek God's direction first.

When I took over, this was one of the many issues I faced. If you have a leader who has pastored a particular ministry for over twenty years, it is imperative for them to step away from the ministry, or that specific church, allowing you lead without distraction. Many pastors do not understand the shadow they cast even when they have passed the baton. I would submit to you tit would have been nearly impossible for Joshua to lead the people of Israel if Moses were still alive.

Moses was an icon, a celebrity. Moses, if alive today, would have a mega church and over one million followers on Instagram. For this reason alone, Joshua had to be confident and secure in who he was. Having confidence in who God called me to be is different from having the confidence in who God called my leader to be. It does not make me deficient. It makes me original.

Every leader carries a different anointing. Moses was anointed to bring the people out, but Joshua was anointed to take the people in. I lost many times because I did not understand my call was different. I had to do what worked for me. This takes us back to recognizing the importance of who you are. Joshua could never replace Moses.

Moses, like the pastors I replaced, were icons. Moses had stood up to Pharaoh. Moses saved the Israelites while releasing ten plagues. Moses opened the Red Sea so the people could cross, brought water from a rock when they were thirsty and had God send quail and manna when they were hungry. The pastors I replaced are irreplaceable just like Moses. But, to make it more complicated, they are my parents as well.

This muddles the ministry even more if not handled with care. My parents have the heart of the people. They have performed miracles, signs, and wonders. They had been there through thick and thin, and every family function from baby dedications to funerals. Where I took a hit was when I tried to prove to the people I could be Moses. But Moses, at that time, was not what they needed and Moses, was not what God was calling me to be. The people knew God was with Moses. The people need to know God is with you. But you must believe He is with you too.

It takes time and trust before the people see you as their leader. The people did not immediately view Joshua as their pastor, and he had to be okay with that. Joshua was not a planting pastor. He did not choose his leadership; he inherited it. Joshua got promoted and no changes took place. It was up to him to help shift the culture. One of the best ways for him to shift the culture was to be the best him he could be. When you are true to God, true to you, and true to the role and responsibility, God will pull on the hearts of the people and change the way they view you.

Joshua 3:7 states *"And the LORD said to Joshua, 'Today I will begin to exalt you in the eyes of all Israel, so they may know that I am with you as I was with Moses.'"* Stay focused, keep a clean heart, and allow no offense to enter and watch God exalt you so the people will know God is with you.

LESSON #2 UNDERSTAND THE DESTINATION

As soon as you clarify what is dead, it is imperative to understand where you are going. Joshua's destination was different from Moses. My destination was different from my leaders. If you do not know where you are going, there is no way you can ever get the people to follow you. Throughout the Bible, we see various figures with specific destinations. The common denominator of those who successfully made it to their target was they all followed the voice of God. The Holy Spirit must lead you so you can lead the people. As a leader you must see ahead of the people. You must see their destination and destiny.

If you do not, you and the people will drift. There is a scripture in the book of Hebrews telling us when people do not pay careful attention to what they have heard, they drift. I cannot overstate the fact as a leader we must listen more than we talk. We must hear more than we speak to make sure we are clear on what God's directions are. One of the hardest lessons I have had to learn was hearing a personal word meant for me and trying to lead the body with it. There will be some personal words from God meant only for us while He will give corporate words meant for the entire body.

When you hear a clear direction from the Lord, it will not be hard to convince the people to follow the directions. As a matter of fact, it is not meant for you to convince them anyway. Cast the vision out there and those who catch it will follow. When Moses took over, the people were in bondage, and yet they followed him. Why? Because he always followed the voice of God. The same went for Joshua, but on another level. It was imperative for Joshua to hear the direction of the Lord because he must convince a body of people there was more after the exodus.

The direction of the Lord will help you to navigate the ship or ark as I like to call it. For those who have transitioned into a position, you are not building an ark (planting pastor), you are turning an ark (transitional pastor) which is much more complicated. Joshua was tasked with the job of turning the minds of the people. He was given the responsibility of aiding the people to realize what they did to get out of Egypt would not get them into Canaan. As a baton carrier, we are all tasked with the same responsibility, to turn the minds of the people. You cannot allow them to reminisce of the past. Phrases such as "I miss the old way" or "It wasn't like this at the old church" are phrases that must not be taken likely. If you hear anything like this, it is time to turn the ark.

If I could turn back the hands of time, the first time I heard one of those phrases, I would have brought correction. I failed in this area repeatedly because I allowed the people to think about Egypt when the focus should always be on Canaan. The example of Joshua aids us in comprehending God has called us to take the people into the promised land. We cannot allow their opinion to overshadow the voice of God. Moses allowed the opinions of the people to sway his mood. Joshua created the mood.

Sure, there were some good times in Egypt. Yes, they had the fish, the leaks, and the onions (Numbers 11:5), and they were probably delicious, but it does not erase the fact they were stuck in slavery. In the past, our church has seen the hand of God move in mighty ways. That doesn't stop God from doing greater now. I learned to never allow the people to celebrate the progress of a season they are no longer in. That season was what we needed then, and 'then' is now over.

We must move. If we do not move, we get caught in the past and the current, while never reaching the future. With Moses, people began to worship the staff. Yet God, was the one who allowed the staff to change their current situation. Do not forget the blesser because we are focusing on the blessing.

LESSON #3 UNDERSTAND WHAT IS DANGEROUS.

As the head and leader, I had to understand this position is dangerous. Not understanding what is dead is dangerous. Not understanding the destination is dangerous as well. But what is even more dangerous than anything else is the danger of not being strong and courageous. This is a position for the strong and not the weak.

There is no doubt Joshua was strong physically. He was a warrior by nature. He knew how to physically fight without a problem. I am talking about being physically strong. To succeed in this position, you must be mentally strong. If you are not, you will not last on this journey. When your leader comes with instructions, you will fold. When your leader comes with criticism, you will fight. Instead of flowing in what God has called you to, you will find yourself falling into places of depression, anxiety, and anger. The enemy wants every opportunity to enter any door left open for him to move in and shake up your life.

Being strong means to be victorious. You cannot triumph unless you are in a battle. In this position of purpose, it will always seem as if you are in a battle. What is key to remember you are not battling against the previous pastor. You are not battling against the deacon board or the person who tithes the most. You are not battling against *"flesh and blood, but against the rulers, against the authorities, against the powers of this dark world and against the spiritual forces of evil in the heavenly realms (Ephesians 6:12)."*

You must be strong and courageous. If you are not, the same people you are trying to take in, will take you back. Be courageous enough to become who God designed you to be as a leader. Do not get caught just doing a lot of stuff. Be courageous enough to do it differently. The biggest fight I faced in taking over a ministry was implementing things the people had never seen or done. I had to conclude that it did not matter who got upset or mad. We will do it differently because we are different. Joshua was courageous enough to follow the foundation that was laid but also to do it differently.

One of the greatest things I have learned is the courage to be God's leader and not man's leader. It makes all the difference. The only thing that changed for the Israelites was the leadership. Joshua did what Moses could not do. He takes them from the wilderness to Canaan. The Moses ' temperament and style of leadership can only get the people so far. If you have not heard anything I have said, please listen to me when I say, "YOU CAN DO IT DIFFERENT – and still be fruitful." You cannot be Moses because you are Joshua, but you can take the lessons Moses left and use them to help you make the difference.

Joshua took the time to sit and extract everything he needed from Moses so he would not fall into the mistakes Moses made. A word of advice to any leader would be to take the time to learn. Like Joshua, God will deal with you differently, but your answer, whether you are Moses or Joshua, should always be "YES LORD."

Remember Moses sent twelve spies to spy out the land. Joshua sent two spies to spy out the land. DO IT DIFFERENT. When the people were thirsty Moses got water from the rock for the people. But with Joshua, he told them to dig their own wells. DO IT DIFFERENT. God gave Moses a rod or staff. Joshua never had one and yet he still led effectively. DO IT DIFFERENT.

How can I say DO IT DIFFERENT without disrespecting my previous leaders? Because even though there are going to be a lot of things you do differently, one thing remains the same. The God who created your leader created you. The same way He spoke to them, He will speak to you. The same way He led them; He will lead you. It just might look different! It is our duty to follow the same God. Adhere to God's commandments the same way you were taught. Employ the faith, the honesty, and humility Moses carried. Lead with integrity and vigor and you will fulfill all Moses wanted to do and what you were born to do. BE COURAGEOUS! DO IT DIFFERENT!

Husband, Father, Pastor, Mentor and Coach are all words that describe Mr. Joshua Caleb Chiles. Pastor Josh, or PJC as he is affectionately called serves as Senior Pastor of "The Life Center" in Abbeville, South Carolina. From an early age, Pastor Josh excelled in athletics and became a standout basketball player at Greenwood Christian and Abbeville High School. Blessed with a full athletic scholarship to Gardner-Webb University, Pastor Josh graduated with a bachelor's degree in Sports Management.

Following college, through much prayer and process, Pastor Josh found his passion to coach and teach. Fused with his undeniable passion for Christ, Pastor Josh has traveled around the world coaching and teaching the Bible blended with the game of basketball. He has also continued his education as he carries a Master of Divinity degree from Erskine Theological Seminary (ETS) and is currently completing his Doctor of Ministry Degree.

Along with pastoring, he serves as the Chaplin at Erskine College. He also aids in the personal success of people as a certified life coach. Pastor Josh has created and implemented many programs that are being used in several states which also reveals his desire to serve, innovate, and create for the next generation.

A trailblazer in every sense of the word, Pastor Josh is married to his best friend and partner in the ministry, Lady Jenae. They have one daughter, Jenasis (pronounced as "Genesis") and a son, Joshua Caleb II.

REFLECTION

"Do It Different"

"You cannot build your son's future on your father's paradigm. Be okay with evolving."

You will reach seasons where things have to die so you can embrace what is next for you. You have to be willing to let go of what needs to die in order to have what needs to live. The death of Moses marked major transition for Israel. Joshua chapter 1 marks the end of a season. He was now faced with the decision whether or not to accept the new leadership. The style of leadership God used to bring Israel out of bondage (Moses) would love the people so much it hindered him from entering Canaan, but the warrior (Joshua) helped them conquer and go in.

In Joshua 1:10, God speaks to Joshua and Joshua goes and tells the officers and they execute. The leadership literally shifts from coddling to warfare. If you are riding in an airplane, you would not want to see the pilot leave the cockpit and start serving peanuts. You would want him to be focused on the flight. That is literally what happened. Joshua stopped doing things that took his focus off the Promise Land and focused.

- The Moses model carried too much alone. The Joshua model mastered delegation. Be constantly looking to get people involved in the vision.

- It is important to know what capacity everyone can hold.

- You cannot be afraid to be revolutionary. The way we used to do it will keep us in the wilderness wandering, but the embrace of the new and different will propel us to our Promise Land.

- Moses worked with a complaining crowd; but Joshua needs encouragers.

6

Rearranging the Stage Before the Curtain Goes Up

Lisa Childers
Administrative Assistant |
Certified Event Planner to Senior Leaders
Atlanta, Georgia

The heart of man plans his way, but the Lord establishes his steps.
Proverbs 16:9

Benjamin Franklin famously said, "By failing to prepare, you are preparing to fail." After 25 years of event management, I have learned things happen you cannot predict. The plan you spent so much time preparing often gets tossed out the window. Imagine going to a play and waiting with anticipation for it to start. It is your favorite play and you arrived early. You anxiously wait for the curtain to draw and for the actors to begin. Unfortunately, when the curtain opens, someone comes onstage and says the lead actor got stuck in the airport and they cancelled the show. I have never seen this scenario happen at a play. However, after planning hundreds of events, I have seen the unexpected happen.

It is easy to get excited for an event, conference, or service, when you have spent countless hours preparing for it. Yet, when the unexpected happens and something goes wrong, you are faced with a choice: will you panic or pivot? When you are under pressure, I want to encourage you not to panic. Let God be God.

From Family Planner to Event Manager

Trust in the Lord with all your heart and do not lean on your own understanding. Proverbs 3:5

Growing up, I was always the planner for my family. My family was spread out across the country and I thought we should come together for more than just funerals. So, I talked to them and began planning family gatherings. I would put thought into everything from the location to the activities. Putting the time into planning those events was valuable for my family.

All of us now share powerful memories and experiences we will hold on to for the rest of our lives. I vividly remember the first event I helped plan. I walked away truly proud. I knew I did an excellent job. It was a women's tea event for my friend's birthday where ladies of diverse backgrounds, ethnicities, and careers came together. When the day arrived and I saw how all my work made a positive impact on others, I was immediately hooked on events.

My passion and interest in event management continued in college and beyond. For my undergraduate studies, I studied nursing, psychology, and sociology, but I realized my interest in events was undying. I went to George Washington University to be certified in event management. As I studied topics like organizational communication and organizational theory, I realized it is not only important when events happen, but how they happen is vital. I began to see how handling an event when things go wrong, or rearranging the stage at the last minute, is critical as well.

Preparing for Change
Many are the plans in the mind of a man, but it is the purpose of the Lord that will stand.
Proverbs 19:21

It can be exhausting to work on a plan for weeks or months and then something inevitable happens. It is called change. Something changes at the last minute. I have learned 'No' matter how much effort you put into preparing for something, you have to be ready for change. You have to be ready and willing to pivot at the last minute to better serve your guests or attendees. The changes may be a keynote speaker's flight being delayed, the power going out, or a global pandemic.

In early 2020, when the COVID-19 pandemic was beginning to spread across the United States, one of the first industries to take a hit was events and entertainment. Nearly every event—whether a conference, church service, or community gathering teams had been planning for months was cancelled. We had everyone and every agenda item ready for the weekend. Then after a meeting with staff and leaders, we had less than 24-hours' notice thousands of people who were planning to come to our services could not.

Six months prior to that weekend, our leadership team advised us to plan on how to handle weekend events in case of inclement weather, or other unexpected activity. In response, we put together an idea of what virtual online services could look like. Although we had a plan in place, we had never needed to act on it. Even though we were planning a trial run, we did not have time before the pandemic came. We had to trust God it would work out.

In that moment, when most people would panic, we did not. We did not panic because our team had already developed a plan for virtual services. We did not think a global pandemic would be the reason, but we were prepared to take our services live the next day and inspire thousands of people.

Learn to Rearrange the Stage

Commit your work to the Lord, and your plans will be established. Proverbs 16:3

When the COVID-19 pandemic forced us to close our church doors, we were ready. Yet, there are many times when you will not be prepared. Have you ever put work into an event, hoping it would go perfectly, and right before the event starts something unexpected happens, leaving you unprepared? When things change, learn to shift, and rearrange the stage before the curtain goes up.

Once, one of my events flopped. In my mind, everything was together. I can plan events in my sleep. I assumed the entire team knew what to do because we had successfully planned this event before. However, all the details began falling apart because I assumed the plan was in place. It was not. Not only were we lacking a contingency plan, we also did not have a solid plan for the event itself.

I began to worry and realize all the assumptions I had made. I assumed the team knew what to do. I assumed they knew their roles and marketing began on time. I assumed the driver would know when to be ready and the culinary staff would have food in the green room. I knew right away the fault was on me for making assumptions and not leading my team well.

Experiencing that failure showed me the importance of communication with my team. When events go right, communication is critical, but when events do not go as planned, it is even more critical to communicate with your team. Your team and your audience will look to you and your leadership, and if you are panicking, they will panic. But, if they see things out of your control begin to fall into place; if they see you remain calm, confident, and excited to do your best to see lives changed in an event, they will remain calm and confident in your leadership.

Stay Calm and Carry On
Casting all your anxieties on him because he cares for you. 1 Peter 5:7

The power went out during an event I was working on. It was set to be great. The PowerPoint was beautiful, the lights looked great, the aesthetics were on point...until the power went out. Thankfully, my team did not panic. We stayed still. We knew (because of our plan) if the power ever went out, the first people to move would be facilities management. Everyone else would be encouraged to stay still. The speaker would come down off the stage and continue to speak. In this instance, it was obvious the attendees were beginning to panic. You could hear the sighs and reactions across the dark room. But, when they looked at the leadership and saw they were calm, they followed the model.

When you are planning something and it does not go well, try your best not to panic. If the members see the leader(s) panic, they will break. Leaders do not have to be perfect, but they do need to model the desired behavior. Another time, we had a speaker flying in for an event. He was scheduled to fly in on the day of the event. Now, if you have ever been to Atlanta, you know with traffic in that city, anything can happen. On this particular day, the weather was extreme. Traffic was bad and flights were significantly delayed. Before the event started, we realized the speaker was not going to make it in time.

Our team responded by remaining calm. We kept open lines of communication with each We spoke with our leadership, and at the beginning of the event, our leader went on stage and made the announcement. We never communicated to the attendees, before his announcements, so the crowd would remain calm. That day, our leader guided us, as well as the crowd, through a challenging change of plans before delivering a message of inspiration to the attendees.

Going the Extra Mile
Without counsel plans fail, but with many advisers they succeed. Proverbs 15:22

In my career, I have worked hard to ensure our team stays together, and stays informed, but sometimes you do all you can to plan for an event, and still your attendees are not happy. A few years back, we had a paid event hosted at a church with reserved seating. When we opened the doors an hour before the event started, the lines were wrapped all the way around the building. When the time came for all the doors to open, I was at the front of the auditorium instructing the volunteers to let people in. Everyone started filing in at the same time and they were pretty calm, except one gentleman.

As this gentleman came in, he tried to sit in the same seat he normally sits in on Sundays. He did not realize this was an outside contracted event and his seat would be reserved for someone else. He was terribly upset. I was asked by a volunteer to help calm him down. This man told us he would tell everyone on social media he would never come back to this church again. He moved to the back of the auditorium, feeling disrespected because he felt out of the loop.

I confronted him and said, "Sir, I understand you're uncomfortable sitting here, but unfortunately, this is a contracted event, and those seats are reserved for VIP ticket holders. I apologize that was not communicated to you prior to coming today. I apologize you did not know we would have special seating. I take ownership for not communicating those details to everyone, and to you." Afterwards, I asked him if there was anywhere else in the room he would like to sit. He said, "No." I looked at him and said, "You know what, you are a VIP to me." I walked him and his wife down to the front to the special VIP section and gave him my seats.

This event was not about me; it was about him. Right before the event started, he was upset and disgruntled. He was beginning to involve others around him and compromise their experience for the evening. We had to think fast and adjust. We kept the focus on the people the event was for. Again, it was not about us. What could have been a disaster turned out to be an incredible evening for this gentleman and his wife. We have events all around us. Even in the midst of Covid-19, events still happen. They just look different. So, what can we do to ensure we stay focused on what is important when things go wrong, or someone causes a scene?

3 Helpful Tips
For my thoughts are not your thoughts, neither are your ways my ways, declares the Lord. Isaiah 55:8

In my experience, these three things have been the most helpful in making sure God is honored and people are served through the work we do.

Do Not Panic Under Pressure. Pivot.

When you are leading events and feel pressure, it is vital you do not panic. You must pivot. One of the most helpful things you can do to make pivoting easier is develop a contingency plan before you need it. Do it with your team. I mentioned earlier, our church was prepared when we could no longer have in-person meetings. We got our team together months ahead of time to hear the ideas and engage feedback as we developed a plan. Our team was included in the process. So, when it came time to shift to online service, we were prepared, and able to serve our people.

Having a plan and ensuring everyone reads it, is always a great idea. Find out, do they comprehend the plan? Is it outlined in such a way every person and every department understands their part? We do not want to expect things to break, but we absolutely want to be prepared for when they do. Having a contingency plan in place makes everything go smoother in case things start to fall apart or you need to make last minute changes. The plan you have will help your team avoid dreaded feelings of panic, even when they do not know exactly what is going to happen next.

We have to trust God with the plan and really hear from him. We have to trust the guidance He has given us through people, through Scriptures, and through planning previous events. We have to trust the greater good is going to happen. We can create a plan, but we must realize it is not all about the plan we put on paper.

Always Encourage Your Team

I have never been able to plan an event on my own. Other people help in some way. The greatest events happen when a team is on the same page. It is when we are all aligned not only with the plan, but with the vision. Some events will be a tremendous success. You and your team will feel like you won the Super Bowl. But there will also be events where you and your team struggle to discover a win because things did not go as planned. It is critical you learn to encourage your team to find a win, even when the event feels like it was a loss.

Like anyone else, I do not like walking away from an event that did not go well. It's difficult when you have volunteers and staff who worked so hard on the event, and you walk away feeling disappointed. In those moments, my demeanor, my position, my attitude, and my tone, all matter. Regardless of how I feel, I need to thank my team. We still have to come together on the final night. I need to appreciate and encourage them. I need to be thoughtful of them. They need to know we did our best, we will learn from this, and we will do things differently next time.

After an event, one of the most important things a team can do is to make sure you have you get together to give feedback. You cover what went well and what did not. When you include and encourage your team in the process, they will feel valued and appreciated even if the event itself did not go as well as you hoped. You cannot allow you team to see you leave an event with a broken heart. Because the next time you have an event, they will remember that.

So regardless of the outcome, I commit to lead with energy and gratitude. I am always encouraging my team and checking in on them. Doing this helps every event be a success for them. Even when a wrench is thrown in our plans, we know we are going to overcome the challenge. And, as a team, we will get better and better, so we are more prepared for next time. A leader is only as good as their team. When the plan for an event has to change at the last minute, the strength of the team will determine how smoothly those adjustments happen.

Trust the Voice Of God And Leadership

The most important thing you can keep in mind is to trust in God and trust in your leadership. If we are only focused on ourselves, when our plans need adjusting at the last minute, panic will set in. In those moments, step back, say a prayer and recognize, *God, this is in your hands*. The Holy Spirit will calm us, and we can move forward through any situation with Him.

As leaders, we can create a contingency plan. We can encourage our team, but our plans may still get stifled. God is the one who will lead us through the leadership moment he has established for us. In my years of experience planning events, I do a ton of work behind the scenes. However, when things need to be communicated or decisions need to be made, it is important to trust in our leadership. Part of trusting God is keeping an open mind. There have been times where someone on my team, or a leader, has said they feel God speaking to them about this event. I have to trust His voice. And if we leave everything in prayer, if we lead in prayer, we are in for a miraculous time.

God says in Jeremiah 29:11, He knows the plans He has for us, and they are good plans. Even when things do not go well, know you have done your level best and trusted God along the way. God will bless you for that. Even when things go so wrong, God will restore you as well. Know you will mess up in time. You will not win every event. You will drop the ball. You will be defeated. How you choose to take what you have learned from those experiences is what matters. Those mistakes or those risks give you lessons for the next event. Along the way, as you learn, be encouraging to your leadership team, be encouraging to your volunteer team, and be encouraging when the plans change.

The ultimate service you are doing is unto Him and not unto them. Everything we do on the stage is unto

Him. I always start every event and meeting in prayer. Through all of this, I know things will change and our plans will go out the window at times. There will be moments we will have a contingency plan and sometimes we will not. Sometimes we will pivot, and sometimes we might panic. The constant is trusting God and knowing what we do, we do for Him. We can trust the outcome is in His hands. Do not panic. Pivot under pressure. Encourage your team always, and always trust in God.

LISA CHILDERS

To define Lisa Childers as an executive assistant in no way fully explains all she does. Ms. Childers is a well-known administrator and event planner, who has trained administrators across the United States and worked to continue her education and training to serve communities in significant ways.

Lisa is best described as "Energy in Motion", known for her dynamic and team-spirited ability to positively impact staff and leaders. Lisa believes an administrative assistant is like the gearshift in your car. All things operate around this well-organized, essential, and multi-functional asset.

Lisa began her professional career as an executive assistant to Pastor Craig L. Oliver, Sr. in 1997. She received a bachelor's degree in Psychopathology and Sociology from Gardner Webb University and a Certification of Event Planning from George Washington University. Her skill and talent for administration is impeccable and her ability to train and empower administrators and staff is invaluable. She works hard to be a gift to those around her through her work and service.

REFLECTION

"Rearranging The Stage Before The Curtain Goes Up"

"There is nothing wrong with being wrong, but there is something extremely wrong with not taking the necessary steps to make it right."

Through the years, I have found out in serving there are usually last-minute changes before every event. As much as you try to dot every "i" and cross every "t", things happen out of our control. In moments like these, it is good to have those who are gifted to execute and never let you know there was a glitch or hiccup. Many visionaries have an image in their mind they cannot adequately convey. The information transferred is sometimes sketchy at best. Once the team pulls together what they think the visionary wants, it is not uncommon to hear, "This is not what I had in mind."

What do you do when you find out you either missed the target in your preparation or you had some eleventh-hour changes in the request? You have to take ownership of where you are and seek to correct it quickly. I have seen people work all night to make sure the first impression of an event was breath-taking. There is nothing wrong with being wrong, but there is something extremely wrong with not taking the necessary steps to make it right.

- You may be tempted to become emotional, but you cannot make clear decisions and be upset at the same time.

- Do not chose to pass blame around. Take responsibility. Take charge. Then, make necessary adjustments.

- Try to factor time for mishaps and correction in your event planning. You will be glad you did.

PART TWO:

THE LOSSES

7

When Life Happens

Michelle Hopper
Administrative Assistant to the Bishop |
Faith Harvest Church
Shelby, NC

I can remember it like yesterday. I was at church serving in ministry like I had always known to do. Children and young people had always gravitated to me and were constantly around. This particular day, a group of us were hanging around after church and one of the older ministers casually with no thought said, "People who usually have kids around them a lot usually don't have children." At that time, I did not think anything of the statement. I did not internalize it. I did not consider it was directed at me. Yet, I would find out and be reminded of that statement years later.

During my process of ministry training, leading up to ordination, I remember my pastor at the time, Pastor Anthony Herndon, asking me what ministry do you believe you are called to? My answer to him was "a teacher." I believed in that moment people were called to the five-fold. During that time, my passion was always to teach; to make people better; to provide information so people could make informed decisions. So, rightfully so, my assumption was God was calling me to teach.

Ironically, Pastor Herndon already knew the answer to the question he asked. I later found out I was not called to teach. He instructed me to assess what I was currently doing and see where I believed my gift would make room for me in the Body of Christ. At that time, I was teaching youth. At that time, where I felt I fit was among young people. I saw a need not currently being met for the youth. I believed until God sent what was needed, there was a need still to be fulfilled Those young people became my passion.

After my assessment, Pastor Herndon asked me again, "What ministry do you believe you are called to?" I realized I was being called to the youth. At that time, I did not know what it entailed, and I did not understand how it fit into the five-fold. For me, being called to the youth was not apostolic, prophetic, pastoral, evangelistic. My paradigm had been so focused on teaching I never considered there was a pastoral gift inside of me. Pastor Herndon was the one who unlocked this.

I was the first youth pastor of my church at the time, Emmanuel Worship Center, located in Oxford, NC. Every woman before me had either been ordained an evangelist or a teacher. This was uncharted water for me. Yet, it was the foundation for everything that was to come relating to ministry for me. So, there I was in 2009 being ordained as a youth pastor. Now remember, in the beginning, I mentioned young people had always gravitated to me. It would be this gravitation that would bring forth some of the most painful experiences I had in ministry.

Lessons:

I am honored to talk about my lessons, my losses and the parts left out when life happens! After getting married at the age of 34, the Lord called me to serve at Faith Harvest Church alongside my husband under the leadership of Bishop Randy Borders. There I had the privilege to serve as the Faith Harvest Church Youth Pastor. I did not even take time off from ministry while transitioning from single life at my former church to married life in a new city, a new church under new leaders. I jumped right in. That, I think is a lesson in and of itself. Many times, we are so eager to serve and be involved we do not take time to pause, make necessary adjustments and re-calibrate. I was in a new house, under a new vision, embracing a new assignment and I was a newlywed. I had a new job and new domestic responsibilities. I was married now!

It can sometimes be challenging to find the balance in all of this newness and still be able to do things well. I remember becoming ill and going to the doctor. My doctor had shared with me I had experienced almost every major life change with the exception of death within a matter of months. This brought on a level of stress manifested as illness. I had to slow down and re-evaluate my personal life, my ministry life and work life. I had to re-establish my personal and spiritual equilibrium.

As a result, I began to prioritize and really seek God asking Him where did I need to involve myself? Being single in ministry and then being married in ministry was a major transition. It is a life changing moment people do not tell you about. There is no manual for it, especially for women in ministry. At times, I literally felt I was slighting God. On one hand, when I was single, I served the Lord without distraction. My allegiance was not divided. My focus was sure and my heart, along with my passion, was fixed on the will of God being accomplished by any means necessary.

When I married, my former perspective did not necessarily change; however, it had to shift a bit. For example, I had to balance the ministry of the church and the ministry to my husband. I had to find time to grow and develop in my relationship with God, my husband, and my new church. My time, attention, and focus, which was once split between my church and God, 'now had to include my husband.

I had to figure out how not to disregard who I was as a single woman in ministry but yet understand what God was bringing me into as a married woman in ministry. I was pressured by others to choose either ministry or marriage. As a woman who just happened to be in ministry and who just happened to be newly married, I did not feel as if I had to choose. Why could I not have both? God showed me I could. I needed to use wisdom in navigating this new paradigm.

Losses:

I started this journey sharing a word spoken over my life not realizing at that time the word I heard would be a reality I would face. I journeyed through the newness of marriage excited and thrilled to be a wife and one day a mother. I felt pressured to start the journey of motherhood quickly because I was 34 when I married. Suddenly after six months into marriage, I was 10 weeks pregnant. There was no heartbeat. The news was devastating but we were reassured this was normal, and it happens to everyone. We were told to just try again.

Nine months later, we experienced loss number two. I felt as if I had been punched in the gut. I felt deflated, defective, deficient, and incapable of having children. Year number three came and so did loss number three. Here we were again serving and bleeding. At this point, I am still the youth pastor. We were at a point where we did not want people to know when we were pregnant because I felt like a failure. I could pray for others. I could believe for others. I could serve others and their children, but I could not have my own.

We moved into year number five having experienced the loss of five babies. I wanted to give up on the possibility of becoming pregnant. I was ready to accept I would not be able to have my own child. I wondered why would God put me in a position to pastor children and young people but at the same time, close my womb? I remember sitting in the back of the church during a New Year's Eve Service faithless, discouraged, and empty. Then, I heard my husband at the podium make a declaration. He said, "By this time next year, we would be changing stinky diapers!"

I thought, "How dare he make a statement like that and put that level of pressure on me when five times before, I was incapable of carrying and delivering a child?" I left service angry. I remembered the words the woman said to me seven years earlier, "People who usually have kids around them a lot usually do not have children." The next couple of weeks were rough, but I had a resolve on the inside to believe again!

We tried once more, and God honored the word my husband spoke on New Year's Eve 2015. Our son, Josiah Benjamin was born the following December! Our son's due date was January 2, 2017; however, based on my history, it was necessary for my doctors to schedule a C-Section at 37 weeks. A full-term pregnancy of 40 weeks would not have aligned with the word God allowed my husband to speak. Remember, he declared in 2015 "This time next year we would be changing stinky diapers." That time was December 2016. God honored the word spoken!

The level of loss I experienced, while still leading in ministry, taught me we must fight for our belief in God. I am reminded of the story in Luke 22 when Jesus told Peter, *"Satan has asked for you, that he may sift you as wheat. "But I have prayed for you, that your faith should not fail; and when you have returned to Me, strengthen your brethren."* It was so important for me to hold on to the history I had with God.

Prior to the trauma I knew of His faithfulness. He had consistently demonstrated His goodness. He had shown Himself mighty and strong on my behalf, time and time again. I remember my Bishop's wife preaching a message encouraging us to always remember in the midst of dark places what God told us in the light.

Through it all the enemy tried to rob me of my faith in God's ability to do what He said He would do. God did not have to open my womb, yet I am thankful He did. He took a broken youth pastor and made her whole. And God not only blessed her with one child but with two! He gave me double for my trouble!!!

The Parts Left Out

As a leader, I served the Lord with gladness even though I have probably written my resignation letter a hundred and one times. There are so many leaders in the Body of Christ who serve while bleeding! To be honest, this is not healthy, nor is it the will of God. There is a reason when you fly in an airplane they go through the emergency management procedures. They instruct you, in case of the loss of cabin pressure, you are to put the mask on yourself first before attempting to help anyone else!

Self-care has become a big buzzword in our current culture. I believe self-care is a function of the Kingdom. God told Peter there was going to be an attack, an all-out assault on his faith. He let him know once he recovered, once he was restored, once he was taken care of, he was to then go and strengthen his brother. It is so important in this space we call ministry. In the space where we serve, we must be sure we are doing what is necessary to keep our cups full. We are to give out of our overflow and not out of an empty, wounded, bleeding cup. Life will happen but we must remember it was never designed to destroy us. We have to grab hold to every lesson, every loss, every win, every failure, every victory, and every disappointment letting them all work for the glory of God. Through lessons, losses and many parts left out, I have served.

MICHELLE HOPPER

Michelle Renee' Hopper was born and raised in San Bernardino' CA. Raised primarily by her mother and grandmother, she graduated from high school and traveled to 'North Carolina on an athletic scholarship. While in North Carolina she obtained degrees in Biology and Nursing from Shaw and North Carolina Central Universities. She is a master degreed registered nurse who has served in various clinical and administrative roles. She is well established as a competent and capable leader well known for her passion and concern for her staff and patients. She is a motivator, a leader, a coach, and a catalyst for change.

She is an ordained Elder serving at Faith Harvest Church in Shelby, NC under the leadership of Bishop Randy Borders where she has served as Youth Pastor and currently functions as his administrative assistant. She is the proud wife of Titus L. Hopper, and the blessed mother of 3 years old Josiah Benjamin and Lauryn Frances Elizabeth. Michelle's parents are Rev. Roosevelt and Yolanda Harris. Her favorite quote is... "Relationships don't end wrong, they start wrong!" She has a passion for seeing people bloom where they are planted and reach their fullest potential.

REFLECTION

When Life Happens

"Trusting God is easy when you have some idea of what He's doing. Life hits different when He's silent and you're clueless."

I would like to say when you submit to being a servant leader life falls in place and there are no more challenges. This is simply not true. When God wants to use your gift, He gives you a stage. When He wants to use your life, He sends a storm. The storms of life forge character and build endurance.

Life leaves scars. You "will" have to preach through tears. It is easy to quote others. Just remember, you can preach another man's notes, but you have to do your own bleeding. There are some things in life you simply have to walk through with no roadmap or blueprint. The mountains inspire leaders. Valleys grow them.

When we hear someone is going through something, before we open our mouths, we should put ourselves in their shoes and apply the grace we would want. It would change our words before we speak.

- When you experience personal setbacks, always seek to confide in someone who can give you sound counsel.

- Know that it is okay to step away and rest. Your mental health is important.

- This is a time for deep introspection and strategizing. Develop your comeback plan.

- Do not allow pride to keep you in a space which you cannot handle in this season. Be about where you are. You serve better when you are whole.

8

I Had to Pray Through It

Nate Jefferson | Founder & Senior Pastor
All Nations Church of God in Christ
Columbia, South Carolina

By now, you have read about the position of servanthood from multiple viewpoints and its multi-faceted characteristics to include focus, resilience, and honor among many others. Many have debated the relevance of various pre-requisites for the successful living of a servant's life. There are no degrees or certifications that can qualify or equate to the most imperative component in the life of a servant. This integral piece to the puzzle of a servant can best be summated based on an individual's relationship with God.

Before someone can commit their life to servant-hood, their life must first be submitted to God through a consistent prayer life. It can further be resolved my life as a servant leader would not be as effective without a consecrated life of prayer. Even in the face of adversity, calamity and conflict, prayer serves as your catalyst and weapon of choice. More often than not, I had to simply pray my way through situations to better understand my assignment.

My first experience of serving began at the age of 18 years old, under the leadership of the late Elder John D. Hairston. The foundation of my ministry as a servant was birthed in prayer. At an early age, I developed a passion for prayer. It is necessary for any person who has been called as a servant leader to have an intense prayer life and not just a prayer time. A servant leader must commit his or her life to prayer in order to know the direction in which the Lord is taking them. This will also cause the life of the servant to be more aligned with the leadership. The word of God clearly instructs us in Proverbs 3:6 (KJV), *"In all thy ways acknowledge him, and he shall direct thy paths"*.

Upon the transition of my Pastor, I began serving one of our bishops in the Church of God in Christ for the country of Brazil, Bishop Samuel Moore. Based upon my foundation in serving my previous leader, I completely understood this new journey and responsibility was going to require much prayer. This newfound position was a humbling experience. It also brought me to another level of exposure with other leaders who were not the kindest individuals at times. This opportunity to serve was definitely an esteemed honor and in that service, as unto the Lord, men and women started to look from a distance with a watchful eye.

I would travel out of the country with my leader and to the national meetings. Because he was older, I had to be more attentive to his schedule and needs and make sure he was where he needed to be. I served willingly, even to the point I had to deny myself and my personal agenda. As time progressed, I found myself serving more during national meetings outside of the country.

Throughout my years as a servant, I have found immense joy and pleasure. Oddly, enough, the anointing on my life to serve and my passion for serving attracted confrontations from individuals jealous and envious of my position. This type of conflict will cause you to intensify your prayer life in an effort to maintain focus on your assignment.

Bishop Samuel Moore was a spiritual father and advisor to our Presiding Bishop, Bishop Charles E. Blake. This presented greater opportunities and exposure to noble positions and areas of confidentiality. It was not until the death of Bishop Moore I realized the magnitude of my submission to the call. On the day of the National Service for Bishop Moore, I was standing in the processional with the family. To my surprise, I was summoned to the General Board's Chambers.

Upon my arrival, I was humbled to stand before the leadership of our church. I was congratulated for my service until death to my fallen leader. Then, a letter was read in the presence of the General Board members from Bishop Moore expressing upon his death, he wanted me to have his Episcopal ring. This gesture was unheard of. In moment, I was advised, although this is not a normal practice, there would be an exception due to my integrity and selfless serving. This was a providential and humbling moment in my life.

Moving forward, I was later appointed as the Overseer for Ecumenical & Foreign Guest. In this appointment, I was given multiple assignments with an expectation of uncompromised excellence. Prior to one of our initial meetings, I received a call from a superior stating I was not a good fit for the position and another person was preferred for this area of ministry. The delivery of this communication was very unprofessional, and it left me with numerous inquiries regarding the decision. Later, I received notification from a fellow brother. I was perceived to have been given too many opportunities and progressing too soon in ministry.

Honestly speaking, I was disappointed by the observations and perceptions of me as I served with a spirit of humility. And the enemy thought the returned message of my servanthood would be the demise of my ministry. He proceeded to encourage negative thoughts about my serve to enter my mind. My desire to serve took an internal blow. I became bitter even while knowing what the Lord predestined. From a reserved place, I would still come to the meetings, but I would watch the culprit walk pass with a cynical grin.

Many questioned as to why I was no longer operating in that capacity. Even though I was hurt and bitter, I still remained true to the code of "sanctifying the leader in the eyes of the people". I continued showing up and being in place. However, my heart had become calloused by the negative friction. My passion was extinguished like a wick with no flame. In this moment, the bait of satan crippled my serve.

According to John 10:10 (KJV), *"the thief cometh not, but for to steal, and to kill, and to destroy, I am come that they might have life, and that they might have it more abundantly"*. The ultimate desire of satan is to <u>kill</u> your purpose, <u>steal</u> your passion and <u>destroy</u> your ministry. The objective of the enemy had been met. My response, though, was to revert to my life of prayer. This was where I gained an abundance of God's understanding.

One day, I was in prayer and the Lord spoke clearly to me saying, "You must let go of the hurt and get to the other side of this. Where I am taking you, you must be whole". At that moment, I decided to be healed and not operate in bitterness. It took me confessing the pain to the Lord in prayer and making the decision to be free from the offense and the offender. That was not the end. I had to go further in examining my heart and doing a personal assessment of why this small fox was destroying my serving vine. I had to pray concerning my feelings about the individual because ultimately, not only am I a servant, I am also a Christian. I want to exemplify Christ in all I do.

I had to pray my way through it! After giving myself to prayer and reading the word of God, I literally felt God root out the core of bitterness and pain from my heart and emotions. The next time I had an opportunity to interact with the individual in a corporate setting, I was able to embrace and serve with a genuine heart and no bad feelings. Hear me on this. While I was praying for God to rid my heart of anger and bitterness, there was no purging of the same from the other individual. Ironically, they were still operating from a place of pride and arrogance.

Months later, I received a call while on vacation advising me the Presiding Bishop was going to be in my area for an event. He requested for me to pick him up from the airport. I altered my schedule, made the necessary changes to be in place to receive him and got him to the event. While in transit to the airport, I was congratulated and thanked for my continued service in taking care of the ecumenical guests of my leader. Then, I was asked if I was still serving in that capacity.

The common side of me encouraged a malice-filled testimonial about what was previously done to me. However, my Godly response caused me to take the position of the victor and not the victim. All that night, I wrestled with not answering my leader with complete honesty. Without fail, the question came up again and I was inclined to divulge the details of the ordeal.

Because of the healing already taken place in me, I was able to present the information with character and integrity. The lesson conveyed and learned was I should never allow the insecurities of others to halt my service as unto the Lord and His people. Months later, I received a call to serve in The Office of the Adjutant General based on a high recommendation. Without reservation, I accepted the appointment. At the next national meeting, I was walking with the Adjutant General, the Presiding

Bishop. The individual who did not approve of my capacity to operate on such an elevated level of leadership attempted to take the elevator with us. Much to their dissatisfaction, they were immediately advised to take the next elevator with the second tier of leadership.

Upon delivery of this message, I stepped from behind the Presiding Bishop within plain view and our eyes caught. The doors of the elevator closed as the individual stood in star-gazed amazement and his mouth agape. At that moment, the spirit of God spoke to me and said, "When you walk in prayer and are spirit led, I will always vindicate on your behalf and you won't have to get your hands dirty".

Oftentimes, we want to vindicate ourselves and tell our side in an effort to have the upper hand. When you operate from a space of vindictiveness, you will not be effective in your call. Prayer has the power to uproot every ounce of hurt and pain. A servant leader must always have his/her heart pure when you are serving leaders on any level.

1 Peter 5:3 (ESV)
...not domineering over those in your charge but being examples to the flock.

Philippians 2: 3-8 (ESV)

Do nothing from rivalry or conceit, but in humility count others more significant than yourselves. Let each of you look not only to his own interests, but also to the interests of others. Have this mind among yourselves, which is yours in Christ Jesus, who, though he was in the form of God, did not count equality with God a thing to be grasped, but made himself nothing, taking the form of a servant, being born in the likeness of men. And being

found in human form, he humbled himself by becoming
obedient to the point of death, even death on a cross.

In retrospect, I believe this situation was God ordained. Every circumstance or trial I am favored with, I allow to be my classroom. This instance permits me to assess my character and integrity while not mishandling those who have a heart to serve. Many times, individuals do not realize the importance of personal prayer and devotion to strengthen their serve. If we look at the life of Joseph and David, their preparation did not begin in corporate settings but in their private moments of prayer and worship.

Sometimes God will place you in certain settings to see the spirits in people around your leader. Your responsibility is to be watchfully alert and postured in prayer. Paul reminded the church at Corinth in 2 Corinthians 10:4 (NKJV) *"...the weapons of our war-fare are not carnal but mighty in God for pulling down strongholds"*. When your service is as unto the Lord, prayer becomes your seat of authority.

Prayer reveals you to you.
Prayer is the compass of your calling.
Prayer provides strategies.
Prayer will give you the grace to handle pressure with dignity.

There have been many life lessons afforded to me on how to endure. My posture in prayer has kept me on my feet. My prayer is to always be in the will of God and my life reflect my relationship with Him. Nowadays, adjutants are more concerned with their relationship with their leader than with the Lord. There may be instances where you may have the right to fact check with receipts and respond with vengeance.

We must always remember; one negative response can disqualify and discredit what has taken a lifetime to build. Maintain a Godly response! Go to God in prayer and allow Him to direct you and not your emotions. I would advise any servant leader to "bathe yourself in prayer and the Word". When opportunities of conflict arise, you will not fall for the bait of satan. Be cognizant of the greater on the inside of you. When conflict knocks on the door of your heart, allow the greater one to answer.

Have you ever had to endure physical therapy after an injury or accident? The first few days hurt because the injury is fresh, and the area is stiff. If you press through the pain, you will regain your strength and range of motion. Your prayer life is the same way. Prayer is the place of spiritual therapy. Here we can bring the hurts and bruises of ministry and pray through our healing. Some experiences will require you to keep bringing it before the Lord. You have to allow Him to work on that area so you can be of assistance to those coming behind you.

Essentially, your relationship with God will constitute your effectiveness as a servant. Based on my aforementioned account of serving, there are multiple points of action. First, you must have a prayer life and not just moments of prayer. Secondly, it is imperative for you to apply prayer to your position and provide your service only as unto the Lord. Prayer strengthens your serve.

Next, you must have a Godly response even when onlookers and naysayers stand by in hopes of your demise. Then, in times of assessment, allow God to search, prune and uproot those things which devalue the character and integrity of your serve. Lastly, continue to pray throughout the tenure of your servanthood. Use prayer to strengthen every area of your life. By praying your way through it, you will see the rewards manifest because of your due diligence in seeking God.

NATE JEFFERSON

Overseer Nate M. Jefferson honorably serves as the Senior Pastor and Founder of the All Nations Church of God in Christ, located in Columbia, South Carolina. He has served in the Jurisdiction of Brazil, South America for 15 years as the Chief Adjutant under his spiritual father the late Bishop Samuel L. Moore and continues to serve the Brazil jurisdiction under the leadership of Bishop Terence P. Rhone.

Overseer Nate' Jefferson is the First Administrative Assistant, Jurisdictional secretary along with the Superintendent for District 5. He also serves as the Missions Director in the country of Portugal under the leadership of COGIC World Missions President, Bishop Vincent Matthews and in the National Adjutancy as Special Assistant to the Adjutant General & National Adjutant Overseer of Ecumenical Guest/ Foreign Affairs.

Overseer Jefferson also serves stateside in the Ecclesiastical Jurisdiction of South Carolina, where he serves as the Overseer of Protocol under the leadership of Bishop Johnnie Johnson and Supervisor Mother Willie Mae Rivers. He is married to, Evangelist Missionary Tarsha Jefferson. He is the father of three children: Talysha, Chase, and Lauryn; who are also actively engaged in the work committed to the charge of Overseer Jefferson.

REFLECTION

I Had To Pray Through It

"When we are out front, our warfare increases. The delayed promotion was God protecting our immaturity."

Prayer matures us. Prayer develops us. Prayer promotes us. Our singular advantage over the plans of the enemy is our ability to offer our struggles to God through prayer. We cannot progress without it. Nor can we experience promotion without it. E. M. Bounds, in his discourse, Weapon of Prayer, declares, "Whatever affects the intensity of our praying affects the value of our work."

Every dimension we are elevated to, requires a deeper level of prayer. In fact, I would venture to say we are uniquely designed for it. Our desire to commune with God and His desire to hear from us is not only commanded, but captivating. There are some situations we can only conquer through prayer. Why? Because the goal of prayer, is not just to invite God into our current condition, but to prove to us we can do nothing without Him.

- Never underestimate the power of your prayers.

- Prayer is all encompassing. It not only frees you, but gives you divine, supernatural authority in the earth.

- God orchestrates opportunities requiring prayer. When opportunity knocks, answer appropriately.

9

Submitting My Skill to God's Will

Pastor Mitchel Blue
Senior Pastor | Uncommon Church
Charlotte, North Carolina

Romans 12:1-2 NIV
Therefore, I urge you, brothers and sisters, in view of God's mercy, to offer your bodies as a living sacrifice, holy and pleasing to God—this is your true and proper worship. [2] Do not conform to the pattern of this world but be transformed by the renewing of your mind. Then you will be able to test and approve what God's will is—his good, pleasing, and perfect will.

Romans 12:1-2, in my opinion, is one of the greatest depictions of human sacrifice and submission we see in the scriptures outside of Jesus' literal death on the cross. It is in these few lines Paul, the great New Testament apostle, begins to paint for us a picture of what it means to be a submitted follower of Christ. It is here in his letter to the Christians at Rome he makes it painfully clear to us there can be no true 'followship' of Christ without a true submission of our lives to God, holy and completely. This is made clearer to us reading these verses (Romans 12:1-2) from The Message Bible:

So, here's what I want you to do, God helping you: Take your everyday, ordinary life—your sleeping, eating, going-to-work, and walking-around life—and place it before God as an offering. Embracing what God does for you is the best thing you can do for him. Don't become so well-adjusted to your culture that you fit into it

without even thinking. Instead, fix your attention on God.
You'll be changed from the inside out. Readily
recognize what he wants from you, and quickly respond
to it. Unlike the culture around you, always dragging
you down to its level of immaturity, God brings the best
out of you, develops well-formed maturity in you.

From this interpretation of this passage, we see Paul is saying God desires every part of our lives to be submitted to Him as a sacrifice; everything pertaining to our everyday existence, He is concerned about. For the believer, this concept of submission is synonymous with who we are. It is understood if you consider yourself a disciple of Christ then submission is your "true and proper" act of worship. It is what you do. However, with this passage Paul begins to expand the understanding of what it means to submit our lives to God.

By definition, submission means to come into voluntary obedience to a person; to bend your will to that person's. That means everything about your existence, you willingly place under the leading and direction of the other party. In the context of this passage, we can say every gift, every talent, every skill, every ability, you place it before God as an offering. You submit it back to Him as a sacrifice.

Now for many of us this presents an interesting challenge. Why? Because some of the things we would label a skill or a talent or an ability, on the surface, do not fit the build of an acceptable sacrifice to God. However, the reality is, everything God gave us; everything he developed in us was done with purposed intention in mind. He told Jeremiah in Jeremiah 1:5 (NIV)

"Before I formed you in the womb I knew you, before you were born I set you apart; I appointed you as a prophet to the nations."

In other words, before you were conceived in the womb, I already knew you; I already knew all I would place in you and I have already placed an assignment on your life. Everything about your life has purpose and intention. There is nothing wasted and there is nothing done by mistake. This revelation is where the journey began for me.

When I was younger, I would often sit and wonder what it was God has given me and why I was wired the way I was. I would often question why my mind worked the way it did. Why I structured my thoughts the way I did? Why I would spend hours upon hours examining things others would seem to think were arbitrary. Yet for me, there was an exuberance in understanding why things were the way they were and how they all seemed to work together. I thought about how the simplest component, out of alignment or out of place, could cause the entire ecosystem falter.

I thought I was just strange . What I did not know then, but I understand now, is God placed in me the ability to analyze situations and environments, as well as map out solutions to multi-faceted problems. He had given me a gift to problem solve. It was not wasted creativity, but something God has placed there intentionally and on purpose. I had the ability to simplify complex challenges and provide solutions in plain language all could comprehend.

It was a gift. What I did not realize with every gift, there is the responsibility to manage what has been given. And not only was there a responsibility to manage the gift; I also had an accountability to the one who was the giver of the gift. Every gift, talent, and ability God has bestowed, is given to us on loan. It still belongs to God. It has been given to us with the understanding it is to be stewarded. And when the time comes, there is an expectation there will be a return of profitability from what was given. At some point, I would be required to submit my gift back to the giver and provide an answer stating what I had done with what had been given.

This model is shown in the parable of the talents found in Matthew 18. Here, the master is planning a trip. He calls his servants in and he gives each of them talents; to one he gave 5, to another he gave 2, and to the last he gave 1. He gives them these talents with an expectation. At his return, the servants would have taken what was given and increased or expanded upon it. The expectation was they would have been good stewards, applied themselves and hopefully made the master a profit.

The parable goes on to say when the master returns, the one he had given 5 to, produced 5 more. The one he had given 2 talents, produced 2 more. However, the one he had given the single talent to, had no production from his talent. He could only return what had been given. Every time I read this story, I say to myself, "Surely he could have produced something. There had to be something wrong for him to produce nothing. I believe this servant committed two faults. The first was a lack of faith. It takes faith to risk investing his talent in something that could produce a return. The second was seeing his talent with a limited scope. His perception of his talent was so restricted, he felt his only option was to bury it.

Gifts and talents are meant to be explored and experience. They are to be shared and enjoyed thus empowering their ability to produce. His inability to see the potential of what was given preventing him from mastering the opportunity provided. I believe one of the greatest lessons a believer can learn is to never limit the potential of what has been given to us by God. When we attempt to box God in, only using our gifts in limited spaces and arenas, we lose. We put ourselves in the same place as this wicked servant; at the altar of sacrifice with nothing more than what was originally given. The truth is, we all will have to face our "altar of sacrifice" moments, where God demands of us an answer to the question, "What did you do with what I gave you?".

For me, my altar experience with God happened in Fall 2007. I had completed my undergraduate degree in Engineering, and was married with two beautiful girls, Zoe, and Kennedy, 3 and one years old, respectively. I had been serving in ministry for over 10 years; from ordained deacon to licensed minister to now ordained elder in the Lord's church. Not only was I prospering in the things of God, I was also climbing the corporate ladder in my professional career.

Prior to the completion of my master's degree, God opened a door for me to take a new demanding role at one of the largest banks in the country, Bank of America. My gift had made room for me and brought me before great men. By all measures and standards, one would say things were looking up right? You would think so, but it is here my world began to shift. I had come face to face with God at the proverbial altar of sacrifice. It is here God asked the daunting question, "What did you do with what I gave you?".

At this point, I begin to talk about the things I had accomplished professionally. I mentioned how I used my problem-solving skills to provide answers to some of the most challenging business problems within my division. I was doing my thing; but yet the Lord was still asking, "What have you done with what I gave you?". Baffled and confused, I began to rationalize. "Well, this is something I do well, but it really does not have a place in the realm of the church. I have mastered this concept, but I do not see how this fit into the grand scheme of what I feel the Lord has called me to do."

I had fallen in the same trap as the wicked servant in the parable of the talents. Instead of exploring the full potential of my talents, I decided to take the route requiring no faith and no accountability. Instead of trusting God to expand my vision; to see more than what I thought were my abilities, I buried them in the ground, thus insuring there would be no return. I had given into the temptation to compartmentalize; to restrict the usage of what God has given for only the purpose I could see.

When we do not understand why God has developed some of the abilities and skills in us, we tend to look at things from a very myopic view. We limit the application of our abilities to the one purpose that makes sense to us. But the scriptures clearly tell us His thoughts are not like our thoughts and His ways are far beyond ours. God does not approach the happenings of our lives with a myopic view. He approaches the circumstances of our lives from a Romans 8:28 view; *"...and we know that all things work together for the good of them that love the Lord and are called according to his purpose."*

In the mind of God, nothing happens in our lives by accident. Nothing happens by coincidence. Everything about our life and the circumstances of our lives are all working together to fulfill the purpose and the plan God had from the very beginning. We are just walking out the process. And there are times when the process demands we submit our skill and our will at the altar of sacrifice; so, it can be conformed to will of the father.

The joy and pain of a relationship with God is often He does not tell us all we have to go through in the process of our skill and our will being submitted. The utopian depiction we would like to see is God showing us the shortest distance between two points, which is always a straight line. However, what God tends to leave out is while there is Point A and Point B, the journey we take is not reduced. This continual progression of Point A toward (destiny) Point B creates what I call the paradox of "the dip".

God shows us what our future will be; what the finished product of full submission looks likes, but He does not show us all of the things we have to go through to obtain it. He shows us the majestic nature of his purpose and His plan being fulfilled in our lives; but He does not reveal to us the suffering (the dip) that is a necessary part of the process. God showed me all I would accomplish at an early age.

As I grew older, He confirmed all He had shown me in my youth, but He never showed me "the dip". He never showed me the totality of the journey and all I would go through. He never showed me the process of my skills being perfected for His use. He did not show me the bankruptcy. He did not show me the foreclosure. He did not show me repossessions. He did not show me the public assistance that would be needed. He never showed me the hell of 2007 and most of 2008; and the toll it would take on my family. But He gave me an assurance if I could endure the process, there was a reward waiting for me.

At the time, it seemed cruel God would not give me full disclosure. But if He had done so, where would the necessity of faith been? If He showed us everything we would go through, why would we need trust Him or believe Him. I now understand it was not about getting the degrees. It was not about completing the coursework and building a repertoire of skills and abilities. There was a duality of purpose in the mind of God that did not exist in my own mind. There was a duality of purpose at work in the will of God that did not fit my will and my plan.

God had to process 'self' out of me and the only place it could be done was at the altar of sacrifice. Any other way would have bred confidence in my ability and not faith in God. Anything else would have given glory to others who were only playing their roles versus giving praise to the master composer of my life symphony. Through it all, God confirmed the investments I made in you were not just for the benefit of secular business. Everything I put in you, was put there with a duality of purpose in mind. I wired you to be able to function and thrive in two realms. I created you to be able to speak the language of the king; and master the intricacies of the sacred.

However, getting to that place required the journey of process. I had to go through all I experienced. Arriving any other way would have caused me to be underdeveloped and unable to sustain the weight of the assignment. God had to birth in me an appreciation for my submission process. He had to sear into my heart a love for the journey. Every turn on the journey fashioned another dimension.

Every challenge added another wrinkle of definition. Every obstacle layered another level of distinction, weaving a tapestry similar to Joseph's coat of many colors. Every mountain and every valley served as another swatch to the brilliant garment becoming my reward. In this process, on this journey was full redemption, full restoration, and another level of ministry I could have never imaged I would see. Thanks, be unto God!

This is what God does when we submit our will and our skill wholly to Him. He makes what seems impossible in our own ability and absolutely no sense in our own mind, to become a living breathing reality. All because we were willing to trust Him with what has always and still belonged to Him. We allowed Him to place His "super" on top of our natural thus creating the exceedingly, abundantly moment that was always a part of His divine plan.

Your submitted to His will is truly the recipe for unlocking the supernatural in every arena of your life. It is through this process of submission He causes us to be able to tread upon the high places bringing what was out of reach in our grasp. I can honestly say my life is the personification of this truth: God's plans are always so much bigger than ours. His dreams for us are always much greater than we can imagine. We can rest in His upon his promise, *"...that if ye be willing and obedient, ye shall eat the good of the land..."*. Isaiah 1:19 KJV

MITCHEL BLUE

Pastor Mitchel Blue is a country boy at heart with tremendous vision and capacity to reach the lost, build people, and serve the body of Christ. He is passionate about building people and seeing leaders discover their hidden potential. He honors the legacy of his school, North Carolina A&T State University, where he earned his B.S in Electronic Engineering Technology. In 2007, he earned his M.B. A, and is working on his M Div.

Uncommon Church is the expression of God's vision revealed to him to compel people to experience the extraordinary power of God regardless of where they came from. Pastor Blue's style of ministry challenges people to move forward in a way that is practical and life changing.

As a bi-vocational Pastor, he finds joy in his career in technology and his free-time as a so-called "amateur golfer". Lastly, he finds immense pleasure in being the "king of the castle" in a home surrounded by his daughters and loving wife.

REFLECTION

Submitting My Skill To God's Will
"Life is more about your process than about your performance."

There are many times I have wondered why God allowed me to experience many of the things I went through. Yet, over the years I understand God wastes nothing. No moment in life is considered pointless, unnecessary, or useless. Every instant, no matter how challenging, every minute, no matter how interesting, and every second, no matter how confusing, is a piece of a greater tapestry woven with love and purpose, by God.

Each skill I learned, is needed for God's plan. Each talent I have, is devoted to God's design. Each ability I discover within me is designated for God's intention. The test is my willingness to submit all of me to God's goal for my life. Therein lies the quandary. Everything in me has God's fingerprint on it. But, He has given me a choice. I can choose to be identified as His, or to be associated with "not His".

- Submission is not a sign of weakness. It represents the strength to know I don't have all the answers. God does.

- While your parents conceived you, remember God 'made' you. (Psalm 139)

- There is no skill I have God has not created an opportunity for me to use.

10

Pursuing My Assignment and My Sanity
Dr. SaLynn K. Evans
Church Strategist
Atlanta, GA

You know the feeling you get in the pit of your stomach when you are at the highest peak of a roller-coaster and it is about to plunge several feet downward? Is it fear? Is it anxiety? Is it just my nerves getting the best of me? Who know exactly what it is? This is what it felt like on the journey to pursue my assignment. I was nervous, anxious, and afraid. I was nervous at being called into ministry because, to me, most people who are called either preach, pastor or minister. I was not a trained theologian. I did not want to be guilty of any spiritual malpractice. This feeling of anxiety arose when I considered being responsible for the spiritual wellbeing of a group of people. It was the unknown I was really afraid of.

What would saying yes to the call of God require me to sacrifice? Would I have to give up my life, my career, relationships and friends? You see, I was a comfortable Christian and an expert at living a lukewarm life. I loved God but I definitely did not want to fully commit to anything I did not know or study. Preaching or working in the church was never on my radar. I have sung the song, "I'm a soldier in army of the Lord" but your girl was definitely not trying to enlist.

Here is my story! I was a classy, bougie, outspoken Southern Belle who was comfortable with life as she knew it. From grade school to college, I lived in the small town of Savannah, Georgia. I worked and spent a lot of time with my family. After graduating from Johnson High School, I attended Savannah State College, now Savannah State University. Both my high school and college were in walking distance from my childhood home. So, when I say I was comfortable, this is exactly what I meant. At that time, my future plans were to get married and live close to home.

Like every other college student, I thoroughly enjoyed my independence, my freedom and hanging out with my friends. An old soul and wise beyond my years, I was the defender, protector, and caretaker of the group. It was not uncommon for someone to invite me to the club and pay my cover charge. I was never a consumer of alcohol and to this day I do not drink. That is not because I did not try.

Honestly, my alcohol tolerance is extremely low, and I do not like the feeling of being out of control But, I loved to dance. I loved the Miami style hip hop rap music like "Tootsie Roll", "Whoop There It Is" and "Scrub Da Ground". If you are familiar with any of these songs, you know why preaching or working for God was never on my radar!

Well, the time had come to move on from "scrubbing da ground". I began focusing on my life after college. The thought of leaving Savannah, my friends, my family and being comfortable was a huge hurdle for me. I just did not feel like myself. Although I was never clinically diagnosed, my days were filled with deep sadness, uncertainty, isolation, and depression It was scary. Life as I knew it was about to change. I sensed it. I felt it. Clearly, I did not know what my next steps were.

Confused about the path forward, I did what I always did and went to work. While some people may be smarter and cuter; here was not anyone who could work harder. As a biology pre-med major in college, I worked

3 jobs: Chuck E. Cheese, Eddie Bauer, and Champs Sports. I was Captain of the Flag Team. I pledged the most dynamic sorority in the world, Delta Sigma Theta Sorority, Inc. Keeping busy and staying distracted were my drugs of choice so I could avoid thinking about my future.

What I did know was, staying in Savannah would be unfruitful. On the hand, leaving would separate me from my family and comfort I had grown accustomed to. Attempting to figure out life not only left me feeling depressed but, led me into a series of bad relationships. Remember, all I wanted to do was to graduate high school, marry my high school sweetheart, be a mother and be a housewife. How sad could that be? In my mind, this was the darkest season of my life - even though I had not lived long enough to know this was not a true dark season. I was not eating. I was not combing my hair; I was not brushing my teeth. I was merely existing, even though I continued to work and attend class like nothing was wrong. My life as I knew it was changing. I did not like it. I was not handing this transition well.

One day, while driving home from class there was an awkward silence in my mind. A chill was in the air. For some odd reason, I remember being hypersensitive to sound and 'noise. I could hear the sound of my car tires on the pavement. I believe my inner most being was aware of what was about to happen. I was going to be leaving the place of comfort and my family. The gravity, the severity of that fact triggered so many emotions. I was sobbing but there was no audible sound. I had to pull over because I could not see the road ahead.

The uncertainty of the days ahead was expressing itself without my participation. I was lonely, isolated, and sad all at the same time. This would be the first of many road signs. God was directing my path and my life's plan was being overwritten with God's plan. Isaiah 29:11 declares *"His ways are not my ways nor are His thoughts my thoughts"*. And, though I did not know it, at the time, I was learning God's blueprint, His methods, and His plan work!

Months of being unsure, overworked and physically drained took a toll on my academic work. My lack of focus affected my grades during my senior year in college. I failed my Human Anatomy & Physiology class by one point. I was angry I could not graduate in May with my classmates. I made an appointment with my professor to discuss why he did not give me the one point I needed graduate. Come on! One Point! I cannot get one point, man?

I arrived early. I sat in my car rehearsing how I would plead my case. I would convince my professor I deserved to be given the one point I needed to graduate on time. I was even prepared to give him the rachet ghetto version of the same speech if things did not go as planned. What I did not know was this meeting would change me in ways I never could have imagined. I never forgot what my professor said. "There has always been something uniquely special about you. You are brilliant, smart, beautiful and you would make a stellar scientist. There is so more in you and I intend to pull it out of you next semester when you repeat this class. I will never give you anything you did not earn, but I will give you everything you work hard for."

"Enraged" is an understatement of how I really felt. This is a good ole Christian book and I cannot inject my carnal thought into this discourse, so I digress (smile). This conversation was the next road sign on the journey to my assignment. How profound. Somehow my professor, who happened to be Hindu, spoke to my future. I never forgot it. He had no idea what his words would mean to me. My work ethic would change for ever. It is my nature to be a really hard worker!

The conversation with my professor solidified the fact no one owes you anything, but arduous work will lead to promotion. Later, this same professor would offer me an opportunity to move to Nashville to pursue a master's degree at Fisk University. Hey, I did not have anything to lose so I loaded up the truck (while the Beverly Hillbillies jingle is playing in my mind) and I moved to Hee-Haw Land, The Music City, Nashville, Tennessee. Remember, I did not really have any goals in life except to marry my high school sweetheart and live in some apartments down the street from my parents' house! Talk about low living! What in the world was I thinking?

My transition to Nashville, Tennessee is a vital and critical part of my story. I matured rather quickly. My mind had to be renewed and transformed to the possibilities ahead. I was physically sick to my stomach the day I left Savannah to embark upon my new life in Nashville. Although, I did not understand what God was doing, I knew I would collide with destiny on this path toward my assignment. Once in Nashville, all I could think about was completing my master's degree in two years so I could return to the land of comfort – Savannah, Georgia.

But right before graduation, I had a major setback with my research project. Once again, it seemed history was repeating itself. Once again, I was faced with the possible of not being able to complete my degree. The grant funds were depleted. I was plagued with the reality of not graduating on time, again. I knew no one was going to give me anything. I had to get aggressive about finding a way to get more funding. One of the lab assistants shared with me he worked part-time at the medical college across the street. He was sure someone would fund my research so I could graduate on time.

So, guess what I did? I marched my small-town self over to the medical college and found someone who was willing to fund my research. I was determined not to fail. I did not know God was orchestrating the affairs of my life and I was completely clueless. The more I progressed forward, the plan of God was deliberately and gently being revealed. While I was excited to find a new preceptor and funding, I was not at all happy about starting a new research project months before graduation.

For almost two years, I conducted research for the National Aeronautics and Space Administration (NASA), but my new preceptor was an expert in infectious disease and microbiology. These were two completely different fields of science. Time was not on my side either. I took on the challenge, without fear, because I just wanted to get out of Nashville. I worked feverishly hard, completed my degree, and had a plan to return to Savannah.

Much to my surprise, my new preceptor requested a meeting to consider my plans after the completion of my master's degree. I did not have the heart to tell him. I just wanted to go back home. I attended the meeting but did not have much to say. During the meeting, he offered me the opportunity to pursue my Doctorate. Doctorate? No, indeed! I did not even want a master's degree. I did not have a solid plan for my life at the time. Me in graduate school for 5 more years to get a doctorate! Umm, that would be a no for me...a really strong no!

Yet, similar to my undergraduate professor, he saw something in me I did not see in myself. He shared why I would be an excellent candidate for a doctorate degree. He shared he never saw anyone work as hard as I did. I told him all the reasons why I was not ready, was not qualified, was not prepared, or even interested in his offer. My grades were excellent. I have always excelled in science. I love the journey of discovering new things, but I did not have good Graduate Record Examination (GRE) scores. Why?

Becoming a scientist was never on my radar and never a part of my plan, so I was not prepared. I told him I would consider his offer and get back to him, but it was a still a really strong no for me. I loved science. I loved studying all the intricate systems of the body and the many mechanisms it has to heal and repair itself. Never in a million years had pursing science as a career was ever a reality for me.

I called my mom for her wisdom and what was initially a really strong no, turned in to a fresh, amazing yes! Before I could share my decision with my professor, he called me. He had already spoken to o the Dean of the School of Graduate Studies and Research at Meharry Medical College. Not only did I not have to worry about my GRE scores, but the school would handle my tuition, books, housing and provide a monthly stipend if I would make the commitment. I met with the Dean to complete all of the necessary paperwork. Eventually, I would find out my professor was the husband of the Dean. God was truly orchestrating the affairs of my life. Nashville did grow on me.

Now, I needed to find a ministry to connect with. I was still a lukewarm Christian, but God had blessed me so. I was compelled to show my appreciation to Him. I knew I was going to need God's help to complete my doctorate degree. There was a popular ministry, literally down the street from the school. It was well known for connecting with the local college campuses. Even though there were rumors flying around the church was a cult, my classmates and I decided to go together to see for ourselves. After my very first time attending, I knew it was where I was supposed to be.

I joined the ministry in 1999. It was definitely a new experience for me. I grew up in a very traditional Baptist Church, where the deacons sat separate from their wives. We said we believed in the filling of the Holy Ghost with the evidence of speaking in tongues. However, you could have a Baptist fit and scream to the high heavens until your church hat fell off; but speaking in tongues stuff was forbidden. The ushers wore nurse's uniforms, had white gloves, white opaque stockings, and those thick-soled nursing shoes. We still covered our communion table with white sheets and the choir, as well as the ushers, marched around the church during the offering. This new experience was nothing like my old church.

This church was innovative and contemporary. It was fun and exciting and most of all, the message was preached in a way I could understand for the first time in my life. I jumped in, feet first and began volunteering as much as I could. Eventually, I was filled with the Holy Ghost at a prayer lock-in. I also became a licensed minister while completing my doctorate at Meharry Medical College. Ultimately, I was ordained as an elder in the Lord's Church. I will talk more about my call into the ministry later.

Here I was finally embracing this scientist doctorate thing and God calls me into ministry. Ministry? You have got to be kidding. In my mind, science and the Church were not even related. Yep, I am crazy! I have to be! Whoever heard of a preaching scientist? I did my research and found out such an anomaly existed. I had enough sense to know I would need someone to help me navigate the uncertain waters of my call to ministry, as a scientist. None of it was making sense to me. I found a mentor who is a brilliant chemical engineer by training and a dynamic preacher.

The same way, I marched over to the Meharry Medical College to find a new preceptor, was the same way I marched right into this woman of God's inbox and asked her to mentor me. Pursuing my assignment and my sanity is the perfect topic for this chapter! God was calling me into ministry, but I was dragging my feet and fighting Him every step of the way. Here are some of the biggest and most valuable lessons I learned when God made a sharp left-hand turn moving me from the right lane of my life.

Lesson #1 - When God calls you, just answer!

"So, you are going to act like I did not call you, huh?" God said, with an undeniable, yet extremely loud audible voice. I had just left my interview at Jackson State University in Jackson, Mississippi, for an assistant professor/postdoctoral position. As a trained scientist, I was looking forward to my six-figure income. Due to past experience, I found myself wanting 'No' parts of the church, preachers, or church people. Afterall, I had spent the last 7 years of my life becoming comfortable with the idea of being a scientist. Yet, I began asking myself the following questions.

> Me: Who abandons a career in science to pursue full time ministry?

> Me: Is this really you God?

> Me answering myself: Naw, this cannot be God telling me to leave the money.

> Me: But God is able to do exceedingly and abundantly for me.

Me: You know you could not find Obadiah without looking at the table of contents. Do you even pray consistently enough to be in ministry?

Me answering myself again: Girl you are clearly insane. You do not even know God well enough to represent Him. You know you cannot preach, right? At best, you are a great Sunday School teacher but preaching... no way!

What would my family and friends think about my mental health if I told them God called me into full time ministry? If I were considered sane before the call, I definitely would not be afterwards. Can you imagine! I questioned the call on my life for years. I would eventually surrender but I was extremely reluctant. I began to recognize a pattern. It was God navigating these major transitions in my life. As an A-type personality, I strive to be organized and prepared. It makes me less anxious and I do my best work when I am not under pressure.

Clearly, God did not care if I was prepared or not. When God calls you, just answer. He has a purpose for you much greater than yourself. You will not know all of the details. Trust me when I tell you there are people waiting for you on the other side of your yes. Do not cause them to be delayed because you are afraid to say yes!

Lesson #2 – Know who you are and be secure in your identity.

While pursuing my assignment, the most valuable lesson I learned was confidence with my identity in Christ. We were made in God's image, in His likeness and He gave us dominion (Genesis 1:26). When God made me, he chose my ethnicity, my gender, my stature, my hair, my physical appearance - all with a plan in mind. You are one in a million, literally. You were born on purpose, with a purpose. You are valuable enough to be granted access to the Earth solely to represent God!

Your confidence should be in God and God alone. Be fully you. Your idiosyncrasies are important, and your personality is beneficial to the people you are called to serve. Be assured in knowing God thought enough of you to make you a visible representation of Him. Whenever the desire to become someone else creeps up on you, reject the thought and remember you are made in God's image.

I heard Pastor Hart Ramsey say, "One of the most important decisions God made about you is who your parents are." They had the perfect blend of DNA to make you who you are. Honor that. Being unapologetically and authentically you brings great honor and glory to the Father. Do not waste your life trying to be someone other than yourself. You will find yourself operating as horrible, distorted copy of an original.

Interestingly enough, my unique blend as a scientist and minister would prove beneficial to the body of Christ. Professionally, I studied toxicology. Toxicology is the study of chemicals and/or circumstances which can have a harmful effect on humans. As a result, it was easy for me to assess where the threats were in the ministry, and subsequently handle it so the Body of Christ could function more efficiently. I identified gaps and voids. I was able to develop a plan of execution to ensure the cracks would be filled. Eventually, I became a Church Administrator and was mentored by one of the best in the business.

Lesson #3 – Saying 'No' in ministry does not mean you do not love God.

Personally, serving in ministry is like being in a brand-new relationship. Ministry needs a lot of attention and I gave this relationship everything it needed. I was available and reliable. I showed up early and left late. I gave more than expected. Working hard was my trademark. I wanted to do everything in the spirit of excellence. Yet, my newfound zeal for ministry and my subsequent inability to say 'No' proved to be detrimental to my new marriage at the time. All of this passion would take a toll because I did a terrible job at establishing boundaries and saying ''No''.

Over the years, I have heard the saying, "Ministry ruined my marriage." 'No' ma'am! 'No' sir! The truth is we failed to sustain the same passion we had for ministry for our relationship. We failed to establish and maintain healthy boundaries. It took years of therapy after my divorce, for me to understand and take full responsibility for the part I played in the loss of the marriage.

The lesson here is boundaries must be established and honored. Marriage should never be sacrificed on the altar of ministry. Never! The family was established before the ecclesia. Boundaries are to be enforced. Boundaries are healthy. Boundaries must clearly be communicated. If you settle for casual respect of your boundaries, you can expect for them to be breeched and violated. I had to learn to say, 'No'.

It was customary for the intercessors to gather and pray for congregants after church. One day as I finished praying with a couple, I looked up and my ex-husband was standing in the line for prayer. He said he came to get prayer to see if the Lord would let me leave church so we could eat Sunday dinner together. Although he was joking, I was also aware I was still operating and functioning like a single woman. Needless to say, boundaries were immediately put in place.

Unfortunately, in some ministries, the culture of leadership does not allow for no. It was an unspoken rule. You do not tell God no when you are called into ministry. It was definitely frowned upon and if you did, you were viewed as not being committed. Resist taking on this negative behavior. A person who does not know how to say no, will not last long.

The stress of "yes all the time" will have you mentally drained, make you susceptible to sickness and leave you feeling depressed and empty! I also saw, it was not uncommon for people who worked in ministry to use ungodly activity simply to deal with the stress. I was infamous for saying no. Learning to say no early is a valuable lesson proven to sustain longevity in ministry. I know you want to do it all, but you cannot. I know you want to be everywhere all the time. It is not humanly possible.

Know this. There are leaders who will allow you to build their ministry and not care for you as a person. Their focus is their ministry. In some cases, if you say no, you may be replaced swiftly. In many years of ministry, I have seen numerous heartbroken, colleagues serving with good intentions abandoned. I have friends who served faithfully to assist leaders yet when they needed help; the ministry was silent. I have counseled many who have experienced "church hurt" and never recovered. For others, all they know is ministry and do not feel like they have a future doing anything else. Left feeling isolated and discarded, they do not attend church or serve in ministry anymore.

We all must honor our team! And yes, we must learn to honor each other. Honor those who serve in ministry. Honor those who help build ministry. Honor those whom God has designated to lead. We are all human. We all make bad decisions. We all have shortcomings. And, we all have secrets. Let us hold each other in high esteem. Let us take care of each other. Lead and care for people in a way Jesus would be pleased. And honor yourself by setting healthy boundaries.

Lesson #4 Forgive Quickly, Do Not Let Offense Linger and MOVE ON!

Be kind to one another, tenderhearted, forgiving one another, as God in Christ has forgiven you. (Ephesians 4:32) Forgiveness is one of the most challenging acts of the believer – especially if you have been hurt, disrespected, and ignored in the church. Sometimes we forget we are all human. We are all capable of being sifted like wheat by the enemy. We are not called to denigrate one another. We are not called to persecute each other. If you are hurt or harmed, address it in a godly, biblical manner. I know firsthand how wanting retribution and retaliation can consume your thoughts.

We can nurse offense and want the person to pay for what they did to us. Acknowledge how you feel – the hurt, the anger, the disappointment, how this emotional blow, especially from a leader, can rock us to our core and shake our faith. Admit this jolt may have even caused you to question your faith in God. Feel everything you are feeling but be quick to hand it over to the Father, and quick to forgive.

Here is what I do know, vengeance and judgement belong to God – not you. I also know forgiveness brings along with it peace of mind and removes the corrosion of anger. As a scientist, I know how our inability to manage emotions decreases the function of our immune system and our bodies to self-heal. Unforgiveness, anger, bitterness, and animosity make us susceptible to sickness and disease. In his book, *The Body Keeps*

Score by Bessel A. van de Kolk, the author reveals how instances like these, can have a long -lasting effect on your physical and mental health. I am persuaded it even effects how you operate and function in ministry.

Many of us know people who have no genetic history of life limiting diseases but yet they find themselves fighting to live. Stress, anger, offense, disappointments affect our bodies, at the cellular level, and cause illness. Many autoimmune diseases, where the body attacks itself, are caused by years of stress.

Cancers, tumors, and other diseases are sometimes a result from harboring anger and resentment all for the sake of ministry. 'No' one in their right minds would expect to have a head on collision and not be impacted in some way. Even if you survive and appear to have no physical injuries, you may have experienced post-traumatic stress, which can impact you later.

How many of us are walking around misaligned, having experienced emotional and spiritual blow after blow while never releasing those emotions or never addressing the stress. My wisdom to you is, forgive, heal, and move on quickly. Do not let friendly fire reduce your life span. No longer can you harbor the spiritual fugitives of bitterness, resentment, and anger. Refuse to drink the poison of unforgiveness. So many have spiraled out of control. Working in ministry is not as easy as it appears. The glamorized version of ministry you see is façade. It is difficult work, and it is not for the faint of heart.

After the initial blow of rejection, forgive quickly and move on. Unforgiveness leads to bitterness. My prayer is you would come out of agreement with rejection, lies, inner vows ("I will never"), powerlessness, fear, self-abandonment, depression, anger, deep-seeded disappointment as well as mistrust in yourself and God. By the power and authority of Jesus

Christ we unseat disappointments and cast them down. We commit to forgiving others quickly because we need forgiveness as well.

Father, we recognize rejection is really the enemy's chess move and checkmate. We cannot allow rejection to nourish us for so long. We must grow from it and look forward to the transition. What is ahead is always greater than what we leave behind – even when it does not look or feel like it. Each rejection was redirecting us to the next part of the Master Plan God has for us. Indeed, what does not kill us makes us stronger. Finish strong! Trust who and what you need is on the other side of forgiveness. Our hope and expectation are in You for our futures, In Jesus' Name.

Lesson #6 – Transition Well & With Honor.

You too have a ministry and a mandate. God has required you to build and have a legacy of your own. You have served your fair share of biblical Moses' but now it is time for you, Joshua to lead your people into the Promise Land. You have been faithful in another man's work and the time has come for you to develop your own. Woe unto you if you spend your life building for others and never build anything for yourself. Do not forget about your own legacy! Woe unto you if you serve others and continue to live in a deficit – financially, emotionally, and spiritually. When it is time for you to transition make sure you transition well.

Be responsible and have the hard conversations even if your leader is not ready. Why? Grief is a process and people need time to grieve the possibility of losing you and how will impact them. Be compassionate about the void your absence means to your leader. Be proactive and ensure all areas are covered, and you have trained someone to assume your responsibilities. It is right! It is good business! And it is honorable! Do not self-abandon.

Do not self-sabotage. And for God sakes, do not remain in a place God has called you out of.

Transition is extremely difficult and many times it will leave one or both parties feeling abandoned, rejected, and heartbroken. You can never be fully prepared for the emotional hurricane accompanying transition. Resist the enemy and do not allow him to set up residence in your heart or infiltrate your conversation. Refuse the urge to speak ill of or dishonor the place and/or leader you are transitioning from. The principle here is, you can never dishonor a person or a place and think it does not affect you or your ministry.

It is in our nature to feel offended when we are hurt. Remember, whatever you honor will honor you and whatever you dishonor will evade and avoid you. Glory is honor coming from heaven and from God. When you dishonor people, you are ultimately dishonoring God. Trust me, you do not want problems with God. Your arms are way too short to box with Him. Choose to honor even if the other party chooses not to. Never forget, the place you are transitioning from was a blessing to your life at one point. Remember, keep your mouth off of the situation, off of the leadership and depart peaceably.

Lesson #7 – Rejection can be a good thing!

Honestly, I did not always feel this way. My fear of rejection was the main reason I did not take risks in ministry. As a woman in ministry there were innumerable times I was overlooked, rejected, and treated differently from my male counterparts. That is why **Lesson #1, When God calls you, just answer,** is key. Never forget it! Because my confidence in God was secure, I took rejection like vitamins. I learned very quickly the wisdom and finesse needed to navigate the tables, and rooms where I was invited. You do not have to worry about fitting in. If God called you there, you belong there.

You have the full permission to be the whole you! Wisdom is the discipline and ability to govern your emotions well. Learn how to manage your emotions. Know when to speak and when to remain silent. Know how to navigate and maneuver in the room. Like Kenny Rogers, you have to know when to hold them and when to fold them. In the face of rejection and defeat, you can rise above it. Make no mistake about it. You may have to have 'strong' conversation with others about their interactions, but do it well, and do it discreetly.

What is notable in scripture is both Joseph and David experienced rejection. In both scenarios, their rejection by their families would prove to be the catapulting ingredient for their transition, or in other words, promotion. The prerequisite of being used by God is rejection. Even the Savior of the World was rejected. *The stone which the builders rejected Has become the chief cornerstone* (Psalms 118:22, NKJV). *He (Jesus) came unto his own, and his own received him not* (John 1:11, KJV). But Jesus, said unto them, *A prophet is not without honor, but in his own country, and among his own kin, and in his own house* (Mark 6:4). Rejection is and has always been a part of the call. Learn to master dealing with rejection. Don't allow rejection to 'master' you.

So far, we covered a few lessons and losses. Now, let us address the left-out parts.

The Left-out Parts #1: Counseling will bless your broken life.

There is tons of psychological and spiritual research on the effects of trauma. Trauma often manifests itself through mental disorders and demonic proclivities. Unaddressed trauma can lead to behaviors like identity struggles, drug and alcohol abuse, promiscuity, addictions, arrogance, and narcissistic behaviors. Yet, counseling has been frowned upon in our community for years. There was a time it was unheard of to hear a pastor or leader openly admit they have successfully taken advantage of therapy.

While many leaders preach about and encourage their members to take advantage of counseling, they often do not take their own advice. We cannot allow ministry to prevent us from taking full advantage of counseling programs, intense therapy, and subsequent treatment programs. We cannot allow preaching assignments, conferences, and ministry commitments to prevent us from seeking and acquiring the help needed to live godly, healthy, holistic lives. Only, when we are healed can we be a healer to others.

I am a fan of counseling – not just when there is a problem – but also for mental health maintenance. Addressing trauma will bring about healing, just as much as a deliverance session. Counseling draws out our compassion to acknowledge our own deficiencies while witnessing the trauma of others. It helps us understand the necessity to extend grace and mercy to others.

Finding a counselor who is licensed and filled with the Holy Ghost is a rare find; but they do exist. It will take the same diligence as it takes to find a great internal medicine physician or hairstylist/barber. You may have to try a few of them before you find the perfect fit. Keep looking. Keep trying. Counseling is important. In the end, your healing and wholeness should be a priority.

The Left-out Parts #2: You are more important than your gift.

I have witnessed many leaders be enamored with a person's gift but not concerned about the person. As long as the gift blesses the ministry, all is well. But when the person establishes boundaries or needs time away for self-care, as I said before, sometimes it is not well received. In spite of the response, you must remember you are more important than the gift. God cares about you, the person! Jesus died not for your gift, but for you.

In some cases, I have observed senior leaders experiencing the need for self-care and counseling. They are supported, extended mercy, and allowed time to recover and be restored. We, the church must care for all the same. The same grace must be extended to all. We cannot condemn, dismiss, and abandon others when they are experiencing the issues of life. The well-being of people should be the priority over their gift.

Sometimes, the church is not good at caring for their own. There are corporations who regard their employees better than the church. This needs to be reversed. We are charged with caring for each other. We should set the example for how we care for people, and not for gifts. The expectation should be the mental and spiritual well-being of all are handled with care.

In the science and healthcare field, there are policies and protocols guiding how a person is treated during seasons of impairment. These policies often include, but are not limited to, the following (in no specific order): an evaluation by a qualified professional; intervention plan; an administrative plan to divide the work amongst colleagues; treatment plan; relapse management; confidentiality as well as a plan for reinstatement or discharge just to name a few.

It is a rarity to see such a policy in the church. And even if there is a plan, oftentimes it is not as robust as it needs to be. We must be intentional in our care for others, during tough times, to include, honoring confidentiality, offering spiritual and emotional support, and engaging paths of restoration. Violation of any of these can contribute to the demise of a person's reputation and ministry. The ministry of Jesus was always one of restoration and reconciliation. One day, we all will have to answer to God for the hearts we did not handle with care.

The Left-out Parts #3: Loyalty during a Scandal

In the age of camera phones, text messages, videos, and "receipts", we have seen more scandals in the church than we have ever seen before. Truth be told, these scandals were happening all the time and they were occurring in the Bible. Biblical text chronicles the indiscretions of Noah, David, the woman caught in the act of adultery, and the violation of Tamar. The generations before us dealt with the same kinds of drama. The difference is older saints did not broadcast matters of indiscretions. There was an unwritten code of secrecy. Most of the times, they were able to deal with the wrong thing in a way, the public was not aware of.

There is a quandary I have with this vow of secrecy. This is an extremely hard yet necessary conversation. For eons, the humanity and carnality of leaders has been guarded and kept secret. I believe in covering, protecting, and supporting fallen leaders. I also believe in extending the same grace to others who may have been victimized. We are all human and we all have flaws.

On the contrary, this new generation is not keeping quiet. Some of them want status and for every promise made, they are expecting fulfillment. If the promises are not kept, they are going public. Until they get it, they will continue to gather intel, save videos, text messages and ultimately, expose you. Either way there is a space where we, as leaders, must acknowledge our shortcomings, confess our actions, and hold ourselves accountable and responsible. When we have made mistakes, we cannot continue to do irreparable damage while attempting to limit our exposure at the cost of someone else's salvation.

I have counseled many people labeled as crazy when they were actually victims. I have witnessed people deemed stalkers when all they wanted was a relationship they were promised. I have seen leaders, who have challenges, targeted by those who would "expose and discredit" them under the auspices of "making things right." Yes, we should cover one another. Yes, we should protect each other. However, we cannot risk hurting others in an attempt to shield leaders who have committed grave offenses.

Here are my questions. Where does a servant's loyalty lie when morality, ethics and biblical principle have violated? Who covers and protect the victims? While loyalty and protection are extended to our leaders, how do we effectively and lovingly handle both? How do we, as people of God, walk this line of loyalty and liberty in explosive situations?

We will make mistakes. Our challenge arises when the humanity of a leader impacts the servant in way it affects their view of God. The reality of a leader's humanity must be balanced with why God called them. God does not choose perfect vessels. There are none. If you cannot handle or manage this expectation, perhaps you should pray and re-consider your work in ministry. Leaders and servants are both imperfect, but the anointing makes the difference. If you cannot honor the person, honor the anointing.

My concluding thoughts:

Every role in the Kingdom, whether servant or leader is critical. They need our support and trust. If you find yourself getting bitter and complaining about your leader, check your heart and determine what your next steps are. If you decide to transition, transition well without exposing anyone. A trusted community of intercessors, counselors, and pastors who genuinely care about people are necessary. Remember, our bodies, our minds, and our spirits are keeping score of the stress, the secrets, the heartbreak, and the trauma. My prayer is both the leader and the servant find their safe space of trusted advisors to decompress and release the weight of ministry.

We do not want the weight of ministry to lead to our demise. We do not want the weight and stress of ministry to manifest as sickness, disease and/or mental illness. May we always keep in high regard the positions we are privileged to hold and keep them sacred. Guard your heart and your mind. Make your health and mental toughness a priority. Grant yourself a little grace when you mess up or fall victim to your feelings. Like every industry, the church has both pros and cons. May we be wise in how we handle both. We can all remain sane while pursing our assignments by the grace of God.

SALYNN K. EVANS

Dr. SaLynn K. Evans is an ordained Elder and has served numerous kingdom leaders as a trusted advisor, ministry organizer and administrative genius. She earned a Doctorate in toxicology but forfeited it all to accept a called into ministry.

Her unique blend as a scientist and administrator has allowed her to identify gaps in ministry systems and develop a plan of execution to remedy challenges. Her life's calling is to walk alongside leaders during seasons of transition. As the Olivia Pope of the Kingdom, she is a ministry consult by referral only. She hails from Savannah, GA and currently resides in Atlanta, GA.

REFLECTION

Pursuing My Assignment and My Sanity

"Don't be so thirsty for opportunity that you drink from every cup handed to you. That's how you get poisoned."

When I finally realized my assignment was to mentor, encourage and inspire servant leaders, I dug in. I studied. I read. I listened. I asked. I surrounded myself with every aspect of servant leadership available to me. I expanded my connections. I stepped out of my comfort zone, shifting into spaces unknown to me, but familiar to God. I humbled myself to receive constructive critique and positive feedback.

Throughout this progression, I realized my assignment and my sanity are intricately bound to one another. As long as I pursued my God-given assignment, I was discerning about what resonated in my space. When I deviated off course, insanity ensued. When I allowed anything in, not related to my purpose, I experienced discomfort, distress, and discord in every aspect of my life. The key to my mental wholeness was the fulfillment of what God has called me to be and to do.

- Everything we have asked God for is attached to our assignment.

- Your assignment may frustrate you, but it will always fulfill you.

- If 'crazy' is apparent, it is not your assignment, it is probably your attachments.

11

At The Table of Restoration

Pastor Ra'Shan Wilson
Lead Pastor | Southside Impact Church
Charleston, South Carolina

I repeatedly tell my church's leadership team, "If our presence doesn't make an impact, our absence won't make a difference." I often use this statement as an expression of encouragement to inspire individuals to observe the importance of leaving their "thumbprint" where they live, learn, work and play. One of the interesting things about "absence" is it is never realized when something ever "present" is occupying the void.

For example, I grew up without my biological father, but never realized "daddy" was absent because my grandfather was very present; he was always there. In fact, one of the fondest memories I have of my grand-father is actually a rainy day. Literally. If you know anything about the geographical region of Charleston, South Carolina, some ports of the city periodically become a river or small lake. If it is high tide, a full moon and lots of rain, you can canoe down the streets of downtown Charleston. Trust me, I have seen it with my very own eyes...and it is hilarious! Ahahaha!

Well, it used to flood in front of the house I grew up in terribly. The water would come up to almost three feet. Luckily, the house was built high enough off of the ground, so the water never came inside. This particular day, my grandfather picked me up from school when it was raining all throughout the night before and all day long. We had to park at the end of the street and wade through water just to get to the house. My grandfather picked me up, put me on his back and carried me to the house. now, it may not sound like much to you without the details of the context, so I will share more.

My grandfather is 51 years older than me. This incident happened when I was in 6th grade. So, this 63-year-old man carried his 11-year-old (husky) grandson through the flood and safely to the house. I never understood how he carried my weight, but I recognized he was the example of the heavenly Father. Whenever the storms of life raged, he picked me up, carried my weight and brought me through the flood back to his house.

With a loving, caring, and strong grandfather like that, it never actually dawned on me my 'father' was nowhere around...until I was a little older. Because my grandfather was so present in my life, I genuinely and sincerely never felt the absence of the man who was my biological father. Actually, I would, only at times, call my grandfather, "Grandaddy". Most of the time, I would call him, "Daddy". I always heard my mother, who got pregnant with me at age 14, call my grandfather (her father) "Daddy." I subconsciously accepted I just...I do not know...maybe I did not have a father, perhaps? Maybe I did not think about it all.

After all the awards ceremonies with no father, the special accomplishments with no father, the referrals, and other times I got in trouble with no father, I think I began to consider, it was possibly normal; I guess. My grandparents did such a tremendous job protecting me from anything abnormal I did not realize I was functioning in dysfunction. I did not even have an expectation of a "Dad" to show up. Well, as I got older, that changed.

I vividly remember asking my mother, "Who is my father?" I told her, "I do not need anything from him. I am almost 17 years old. I am fine without any support —financial, moral, emotional or in any other manner. I simply want to know who he is and what he looks like; I want to be able to talk to him and ask him health questions and just see what he is like. That is all." This conversation stretched out over the course of several weeks. I did not ask every day, but I brought up the subject often. Finally, she gave me a name. Interestingly enough, it was a familiar one.

Wait! "Him?", I pondered. So (you may want to get some popcorn for this) my mother and one of my aunts (two sisters) dated two brothers. Well, eventually, my mother and the brother she dated broke up. However, my aunt stayed with other brother for well over 20 years. She was my favorite maternal aunt, and I was with her often. Her two children were not only first cousins to me, but we grew up like siblings. I called the man "Uncle". His family became my extended family. I spent considerable time with my aunt, the man she was with, my two cousins and even my aunt's "in-laws" for years. We all became close. I called my Uncle's mother, "Grandma". I called his sisters, "Aunt" and I called his brother, "Uncle" — the same brother who dated my mother before I was born.

When my mother gave me the name of the man she said was my father, my immediate response was, "Huh? But I thought he was my uncle...?" I was numb for a moment. The man I perceived as an uncle for years is not my uncle? I guess I could easily get pass that part. However, he......is.......my.......father.......??? I was in shock. I was excited to learn more about him, but nervous about the dynamic of the relationship shifting. I mean, he served the country in a branch of the military, was living out of state and married to a gorgeous woman with a beautiful daughter who I, of course, thought was my cousin. Now, I am hearing she is my sister. I was simply in shock.

I believe my Granny's spirit of peace and grace rested on me in many seasons throughout my life because I was not mad. I was not angry. I did not cry. I was, however, confused which was to be expected. Well, the big day came. I was sure his wife and other members of the family would have wanted to be certain of these speculations, so we agreed to have a DNA test done. Tick, tock - tick, tock - tick, tock...we were to receive the results by mail. I waited and waited and waited and waited some more. I was steadfastly looking for what I thought would create a framework of understanding for me. I was not seeking closure. On the contrary, I sought access. I was looking for an open door.

I wanted to know who my father was. No back child support. For what? I was almost an adult and my grandparents did a yeoman's job raising me. They took exceptionally loving care of me and reared me in the fear and in the admonition of the Lord. I simply wanted to just know. Guess what? I came home one evening! I got the results back! I opened the envelope! I was shocked all over again. He was NOT my father. How could this be? Hold on. What was happening to me. For a moment, I felt defeated. How would I start over? Where would I start? I thought, "Maybe it was a bad to look into it anyway." I did not know.

I am writing this passage as a 35-year-old man, married with children and I still do not know who my biological father is. I often wondered, where would my life be if my father was in it? I pondered if the lesson on the "birds and the bees" would have been different if my father taught it to me. I contemplated would certain tendencies and been disciplined if I knew ahead of time, through my father. I had so many thoughts. So many thoughts.

Now, as you continue to read, please, allow me to be clear of two things. First, the sentiments I share are not an indictment on my grandfather. He went above and beyond the call of duty. He showed me the epitome of a hardworking, committed, strongman. I saw my grandfather defy the law of gravity to provide for the household I grew up in. Any stupid choices I made were simply stupid choices I made.

Secondly, this is not an indictment on the absence of my father (whoever he may be). God's grace allowed me to successfully navigate through every season of my life; even the seasons I caused were by making mistakes or bad decisions. This is, however, about me. It is an attempt to show you the reality of issues and idiosyncrasies which develop in your adulthood because they were never defeated in your childhood.

For me, this void created a vacuum; a vacuum that brought a spiritual entity into a biological place. It caused me to take a component which should have been devoted to the spirit and allow it to occupy the natural. What am I talking about? I am referring to the concept of spiritual fathers. While I believe having a spiritual father is certainly a Biblical principal, there is a catch. Unhealed sons often become broken fathers; and broken sons develop biological expectations on spiritual fathers.

This is what happened to me. I joined a church in my late teens. I am proud to say I stayed a member of that one church for 15 years, until I was SENT to pastor another church. While I did my best to transition in honor and humility, the truth of the matter is, I was transitioning in the first place because I was subconsciously expecting my spiritual father to be my natural dad. I only wonder how many more men (or women) in church have had this same challenge. What do you do? How do you deal with it? What happens when leaders attempt to genuinely father individuals who's submission and expression of honor is an outward demonstration to fill a void both parties are unaware of?

I think I have another way I could try this. Let me give you the perspective of a well-known Biblical character, but from a unique perspective. He is one of the greatest kings who ever walked the face of the earth, When you get an opportunity, read Psalm 69 in its entirety. For now, I will highlight a few verses to help us see the bigger picture. Here is the Message Translation of the Bible:

[1] God, God, save me! I'm in over my
head, [2] Quicksand under me, swamp water
over me; I'm going down for the third time.
[3] I'm hoarse from calling for help, bleary-eyed
from searching the sky for God. [4] I've got
more enemies than hairs on my head; Sneaks
and liars are out to knife me in the back.
What I never stole must I now give back?...

[7] Because of you I look like an idiot, I walk
around ashamed to show my face.[8] My brothers
shun me like a bum off the street; [9] My family
treats me like an unwanted guest. [10] When I
poured myself out in prayer and fasting, All it
Got me was more contempt. [11] When I put on a
sad face, They treated me like a clown.[12] Now
drunks and gluttons Make up drinking songs
about me. [13] And me? I pray. God, it's time for
a break! God, answer in love! Answer with
your sure salvation!...

[18] Come close, God; get me out of here. Rescue
me from this deathtrap. [19] You know how they

kick me around—Pin on me the donkey's ears,
the dunce's cap.[20] I'm broken by their taunts,
Flat on my face, reduced to a nothing. I
looked in vain for one friendly face. 'No one.
I couldn't find one shoulder to cry on.
[21] They put poison in my soup, Vinegar in
my drink.

Through no apparent cause of his own, he is surrounded by enemies who wish to cut him down; even his own brothers are strangers to him, ravaging and reviling him. Pay close attention to verse 8. He shares the ill and abusive treatment received by his own family. The King James Version of the Bible does not say, "my brothers." It actually says, "my mother's children." The writer is face to face with feelings of abandonment in such a way he can no longer sense the family bond between his brothers and refers to them as the children of his mother instead of identifying them as siblings.

This psalm describes the life of a poor, despised, and lowly individual. It is written by the one who lacks even a single friend to comfort him according to verse 20. It is the voice of a tormented soul who has experienced untold humiliation, suffering anguish and utter disdain. In my early 20s, I remember preaching a sermon where I said, "The enemy does not want you to be saved from grace. He does not want you to grow in grace. He wants you to fall from grace and become a disgrace, but by God's grace you can make it."

Well, for the individual described in this psalm, "disgrace" seems to be an understatement when trying to explain the pain of what he feels. Amazingly, this is the pen and voice of the mighty King David; the righteous and beloved servant of God. While King David was feared and awed by all, he had many challenges throughout his life. But at what point did this great man feel so alone, so disgraced, and so undeserving of love and friendship?

What was it that caused King David to face such an intense ignominy, to be shunned by his own brothers in his home, to be frowned upon by the Torah sages who sat in judgment at the gates and even by the drunkards on the street corners who whispered negative things about him as he walked by? What had he done to arouse such ire and contempt? Why was he so alone? Why did he feel as if he was isolated in the midst of a crowd? The realization of having many around you, but not necessarily for you is a hard pill to swallow.

I know that feeling of loneliness. I know what it feels like to recognize one cannot change the outcome of a situation, and you are left with isolation, separation, and exclusion as your companions. Ever felt that way? This psalm, in which David passionately gives voice to the heaviest burdens of his soul, refers to a period of twenty-eight years. It is the lyrical content of this musical composition translates the process of his life from his earliest childhood until he was coronated as king of Israel by the prophet Samuel.

David, first of all, was born into the illustrious family of Jesse, in Bethlehem and was of the Tribe of Judah. David's father was a farmer, breeder, and owner of sheep. Ancient biblical records suggest Jesse actually served as the head of the Sanhedrin (supreme court of Torah law) during his time. Apparently, David's father was one of the most distinguished leaders of his generation. Who would not want a father like this?

David was the youngest in his family, which included seven other illustrious, handsome, and charismatic brothers. Yet, when David was born, this prominent family greeted his birth with utter derision and contempt. David describes quite literally in the King James Version of Psalm 69:21, "I was a foreigner to my mother's sons...they put gall in my meal and gave me vinegar to quench my thirst." He was rejected, ostracized, and castigated from his own blood. He was abandoned, neglected and unwanted. Sounds familiar? Have you ever felt any of these ways? Do you know anyone who has?

Only one individual throughout David's youth was pained by his unjustified plight and felt a deep and unconditional bond of love for the child whom she alone knew was undoubtedly pure; David's mother, Nitzevet bat Adael. If you decide to look for David's mother's name in the Bible, you will not find it there. It is found in the Talmud. The Talmud is the central text of Rabbinic Judaism and the primary source of Jewish religious law and Jewish theology. It is a diverse collection of writings, containing full account of civil and religious laws and commentary of the Jewish people.

Nitzevet felt the intensity of her youngest child's pain and rejection as her own. Torn and anguished by David's unwarranted degradation, yet powerless to stop it, Nitzevet stood by the sidelines, in solidarity with him. She shunned herself, as she too cried rivers of tears, awaiting the time when restoration was received. The challenge was, it would take twenty-eight long years of assault and rejection, suffering and degradation until this redemption would finally materialize.

Now, unless these people were simply evil (and we know Jesse was a righteous man), there has to be a reason for their actions toward David. Why was young David so reviled by his brothers, other family members and people of the city? To understand the hatred directed toward David, we need to investigate the inner workings behind the events, the secret episodes not recorded in the prophetic books but are alluded to in Midrashim (a compilation of ancient commentary on part of the Hebrew scriptures, attached to the Biblical text). Stay with me. I am going somewhere. From a genealogical perspective, David's father, Jesse, was the grandson of Boaz and Ruth. It appears, Jesse, after several years of marriage to his wife, Nitzevet, and after having raised several virtuous children, began to entertain personal doubts about his ancestry.

His grandmother, Ruth, was a convert from the nation of Moab, as related in the biblical book of Ruth. During Ruth's lifetime, many individuals were doubtful about the legitimacy of her marriage to Boaz. She was converted, changed, and living a brand-new life, but it was difficult for individuals to let her past die. Sound familiar? Everything arising in your future is automatically associated with your past in the minds of those who fail to let go of what was. I call these individuals 'salty'. Why? They cannot stop focusing on what is behind. Ask Lot's wife (Genesis 19).

So, Jesse upholds, supports, and defends the Torah (Hebrew Law). However, the Torah specifically forbids an Israelite to marry a Moabite convert, since this is the nation that cruelly refused the Jewish people passage through their land, or food and drink to purchase, while they wandered in the desert after being freed from Egypt. Boaz and the sages understood this law as forbidding intermarriage (specifically) with converted male Moabites (the ones responsible for the cruel conduct), while exempting female Moabite converts.

Therefore, the marriage was legit! Most likely, with his marriage to Ruth, Boaz hoped to clarify and publicize this law. It is recorded Boaz died the night after his marriage with Ruth. Who would stand to explain the legitimacy of their union? While it was unfortunate Boaz died the night after his wedding and was unavailable to explain the clause in the law, Ruth conceived that same night, after the wedding. Subsequently, she gave birth to their son Obed, the father of Jesse. Time would show the doubters were wrong. Once Jesse and his offspring were born, their righteous conduct and prestigious positions would prove the legitimacy of their ancestry. It was impossible men of such caliber could have descended from a forbidden union.

However, later in life doubt apparently gripped Jesse's heart. What if the doubters were right? What if he was not the man he, his family or even his community thought he was? His integrity compelled him to action. If Jesse's status was questionable, he was not permitted to remain married to Nitzevet, a veritable Israelite. Disregarding the personal sacrifice, Jesse decided the only solution would be to separate from her and no longer engage in marital relations. All seven of his children were aware of this separation.

After a number of years, Jesse began to long for a child whose ancestry would be unquestionable. His plan was to engage in sexual relations with his Canaanite maidservant. The maidservant was also aware of the anguish of her mistress, Nitzevet. She knew Nitzevet's (Jesse's wife) longed to be with her husband and wanted more children as well. According to Josephus, and other Jewish historical writings, the maidservant secretly approached Nitzevet and informed her of Jesse's plan. She advised "Let us learn from your ancestresses and replicate their actions. Switch places with me tonight, just as Leah did with Rachel". Nitzevet took the place of her maidservant and conceived, while Jesse remained completely unaware of the switch.

After three months, Nitzevet's pregnancy became obvious. Incensed and outraged, according to the law (Lev. 20:10) her sons wished to kill their adulterous mother and the "illegitimate" fetus she carried. Nitzevet, for her part, would not embarrass her husband by revealing the truth of what had occurred. Like her ancestress Tamar, who prepared to be burned alive rather than embarrass Judah, Nitzevet chose a vow of silence. Have you ever had a time, in your life, when you had to hold your peace, take a vow of silence, and swallow a heap of "hush" when you could have said something to clear your name?

Unaware of the truth behind his wife's pregnancy, but having compassion on her, Jesse ordered his sons not to touch her. "Do not kill her! Instead, let the child who will be born be treated as a lowly and despised servant. In this way everyone will realize his status is questionable and, as an illegitimate child, he will not marry an Israelite." From the time of his birth onwards, Nitzevet's son, David, was treated by his brothers as an abominable outcast. Noting the conduct of his brothers, the rest of the community assumed this youth was a treacherous sinner full of unspeakable guilt.

David was not assigned as a shepherd boy because he simply liked sheep. He was given the task of shepherd because they hoped a wild beast kill him while he was performing his duties. Sadly, it was for this reason he was sent to pasture in dangerous areas full of lions and bears. And, yet when a lion and a bear did indeed attack him, he prevailed. On the infrequent occasions David would return from the pastures to his home in Bethlehem, he was shunned by the townspeople. If something was lost or stolen, he was accused as the natural culprit, and ordered, in the words of the Psalm 69, to "repay what I have not stolen."

I now understand, when I read Psalm 23 why David had no relationship with his father so he could not relate to God as a son. At the time, he had no reference to say, "The Lord is my Father." However, he could relate to God as a sheep. Therefore, he said, "The Lord is my Shepherd..." David was not even allowed to sleep at home in a bed. He slept outside with the sheep. Maybe that why he said, "The Lord makes me lay down in green pastures." Wow! He grows up thinking he is the son of an adulterous relationship. Perhaps this is what made him pray in Psalms 51: "Behold I was shaped in iniquity and in sin did my mother conceived me." But restoration was and is inevitable.

We are first introduced to David when the prophet Samuel is commanded to go to Bethlehem and anoint a new king to replace the rejected King Saul (1 Samuel 16). When Samuel arrives, the elders of the city come out to greet him. Nervous at this unusual and unexpected visit, the elders feared Samuel had heard about a grievous sin taking place in their city. Perhaps he had come to rebuke them over their behavior toward the despised shepherd boy, living in their midst.

Samuel declared; however, he had come in peace, and asked the elders, Jesse, and his sons, to join him for a sacrificial feast. As an elder, it was natural for Jesse to be invited; but his sons were inexplicably invited also. Unknown to them, Samuel would anoint the new king of Israel at this feast. Yet, the only thing revealed to the prophet, at this point, was the new king would be a son of Jesse. Jesse had all seven sons pass before Samuel. Samuel said to Jesse, "God has not chosen any of them." It makes sense why Jesse did not call David to the feast. Why would he? The prophet asked for all of his sons. If he did not believe David was his, of course he would not invite him. In essence, Samuel did not only show up to be a prophet, but he also showed up to be a paternity test!

Finally, Samuel is basically like (in my urban translation), "Yo, J, so...you ain't got 'No' more sons? At all? None? Nowhere?   Jesse, still under the impression David is "the milkman's baby", basically replies, Hmmmm, I mean...well, actually.....like, it's kinda complicated." So, there is another lil guy, but I mean...he can't be king tho; besides, he's tending to the sheep." Trust me, there are individuals who simply do not want you to make it. In fact, I submit, most of your challenges come from individuals who are not mad because you are "it", they are mad because you are "it" and they are not.

So, Samuel said to Jesse, "Send for him!" God is sending people to send for you! I can feel it as I write, and I pray you can feel it as you read. When you are God's choice, His demand of your life draws you or drives you out of obscurity. His timing is always perfect. The key is to be faithful where you are. It was painful, David was faithful. He was a faithful shepherd and a faithful sheep. Your name is about to be called. As soon as Samuel saw David, he stood and, at God's command, anointed him king.

Guess what? This happened in the presence of Jesse and his brothers. I love the fact God has a way to "prepare a table [before] you in the presence of your enemies." (Psalm 23) In that context, the word "before" is not a place or location. It is an adverb of time meaning prior to your arrival. The table was set "before" David arrived at the feast. As for David's mother, twenty-eight long years of silence in the face of humiliation were finally ending.

At last, all would see the lineage of her youngest son was pure and undefiled by any blemish. Finally, the anguish and humiliation she and her son had borne would come to an end. It is said David eventually wrote a prophetic song highlighting his mother's words to her other sons the day David was anointed: "The stone that was reviled by the builders has now become the cornerstone!" (Psalms 118:22) Humbled, David's brothers responded, "This has come from God; it was hidden from our eyes" (Psalm 118:23).

After David lost so much — his dignity, his reputation, his influence...and so many other things, this one moment restored it all. See. The blood secures redemption, but the oil ensures restoration. Now, contrary to widely held belief, restoration is not when you get back what you lost. Restoration is when you get back what you would have had if you had never lost anything at all. In other words, when God restores you, He does not put you back where you were. He puts you where you would have been had you never been knocked off kilt. God wants you to submit to the process and the plan He allows. It takes total trusting in God's will.

Those moments I felt dejected and abandoned by my Father, were worth God's incredible moment of restoration. Look at it this way. To "store" means to reserve; to keep or accumulate for future use. Therefore, to "re-store", in essence, means to reserve once more; to keep again. If God can reserve me, restore me, He can...well, wait. Please, let me use emphasis so you understand: If God can reserve and restore ME, trust me, that same God has got you too! There is a place of 'future use' God has for us, after RESTORATION!

RA'SHAN WILSON

Rashan Lamar Wilson is a native son of Charleston, South Carolina. He founded Impact Church, based in the historic district of his hometown, in spring of 2015. In December of 2018, Impact Church and Southside Baptist merged to become Southside Impact Church — endeavoring to be a multi-cultural, family oriented, trans-generational Christian community that empowers individuals to reach their fullest potential in life through Christ.

Rashan is a highly sought-after author, motivational speaker, and evangelist. He is a meek, humble, grace-filled example of one man's quest for truth. For his pioneering leadership and example to the city, he was given "The Key To The City" by Charleston's Mayor John Tecklenburg October 21, 2019. He has received countless community awards, certificates, and expressions of recognition for his work and labor in his community.

He has been the in-studio guest for radio and television talk shows that have invited him to discuss today's most important topics and issues. His three-dimensional goal in ministry and life is to "dig wells the whole city can drink from, building bridges everyone can cross and create tables where everyone can sit." Rashan is married to the former Dashonna Marie Bruton, and their children (Jada, Khloe, Savannah, Caleb & Joshua) are all tremendously gifted, talented, and blessed.

REFLECTION

At The Table of Restoration

"If it feels like midnight, remember that midnight is the first hour of a new day."

Restoration is an ideal that has always amazed me. It began with my deciding to accept Jesus into my life. The fact the one, who was God in flesh, made a conscious decision to give His life for me is incredible; simply to restore me. Even more extraordinary, was the realization "restoration" was His prime objective.

Imagine living a life of guilt and shame, being ostracized, ridiculed, and persecuted because of a decision someone else made. Someone else established how we would be perceived and recognized. Someone else shaped and influenced others to interact with us a certain way. Then, restoration. Because none of it was who we truly were. None of it was accurate. Their assessment of us was erroneous. We were and are so much more.

- Everything you have experienced has prepared you for your next move.

- There can be no restoration without robbery. Restoration puts you in position for elevation and promotion. It lets the enemy know his theft was unsuccessful.

- Once you reach the place of restoration, stay there.

12

Serving Through The Death of My Pastor

Elder Roger Hutton
Executive Board Member | Evangel Fellowship COGIC
Greensboro, NC

The journey began on February 2nd, 1982, in a light drizzling rain. Bishop Otis Lockett Sr. left his home in Cincinnati, Ohio to come to Greensboro, North Carolina with only a green suitcase and his faith. Little did he know at that time Evangel Fellowship Church of God in Christ would be in that suitcase. His loving wife Barbara and his three beautiful children, Faith, Otis Jr, and Joshua would also be in that suitcase along with a loving host of relatives and friends who would come to know Christ as a result of his influence.

He was a true servant of God, pastor, husband, father, mentor, and one of the most influential leaders of our times. He was a holy man, a good man and one of great character. He did not shy away from speaking the truth no matter if it stepped on your toes or not. He wanted the best out of people, and he did not mind pushing you to excellence. He was far more interested in a developing Christ-like character in you than your comfort or how the world defines success. In fact, he used to say success was knowing God; what he desires for my life; and sowing seeds to bless others.

As tough as Bishop could be, you always knew he loved and believed in you. Even when you made mistakes, he was there to encourage you and push you to know God for yourself. He was a servant. He was there to minister to whatever need you had. Matthew 20:28

says *"For even the son of man came not to be served but to serve others and to give his life as a ransom for many."* He lived that way until the day he left this earth.

Bishop Lockett gave me my first bible. It was an Open Bible which provided scripture with references and centered around the belief in the Holy Spirit. Bishop believed in the principals of the Open Bible, which was to make disciples, develop leaders, and plant churches. When he went home to be with the lord, he had led countless men and women to Christ and planted over 25 churches.

One day I was reading the Open Bible and saw Judges 20:16. It stated, *"among all this people there were seven hundred chosen men lefthanded; everyone could sling stones at a hair breadth, and not miss"*. I thought, that is interesting, I am left-handed. I continued to read and found Samuel 21:20 which stated, *"And there was yet a battle in Gath, where was a man of great stature, that had on every hand six fingers, and on every foot six toes, four and twenty in number; and he also was born to the giant"*. I was born the same way with six toes and six fingers. At that point I started believing God had a message for me. I was not sure what it was at the time, but I felt He was grooming my life for something greater than I had ever experienced.

Bishop taught me how to be a man of character, one who loved God, and loved the people of God. When I first met him, I immediately liked him. The first thing I noticed about him was how he did not just preach the word of God, but he lived it. This thing was real to him and he got excited when he talked about Christ. That inspired me, so I started hanging out with him and talking to him every chance I got. I would ask him a lot of questions and what he thought about certain things.

I was still green in the faith and was working on my own character. I did not really know how to walk in my calling. I was not even sure what a calling meant. I did know I wanted to be more like this man I was coming to know as a pastor and friend. I wanted to benefit him as much as he was benefiting me, so I started serving; first in Sunday school, then as his adjutant. Where he went, I followed. He was such an encourager. I began to mirror what he was teaching me, and I started to encourage him.

Earlier, I mentioned he was a visionary, so he would often share his dreams concerning his family and the family of Evangel Fellowship. I remember one time when he saw some land he wanted to purchase. I told him we could do it and I believed God would help us get the land he wanted. I would encourage him every chance I got regardless of what the circumstances looked like. Even in the earlier days with him, he was strengthening my faith when I did not even realize it. Someone asked me, "What was the most important thing Bishop had taught me?". My answer was how to have faith in God.

Two of my favorite scriptures is Hebrews 11:1 *"Now faith is the substance of things hoped for, the evidence of things not seen"* and Mark 11:24 *"What things soever ye desire, when ye pray, believe that ye receive them, and ye shall have them"*. I would meditate on those scriptures until they got in my spirit and became how I lived my life. I remember one of the first times I relied on my faith. My beautiful wife Annette and I already had two sons-Winfred Roger Jr. and James. Annette was pregnant and we both wanted a girl, so I began praying to God for a girl. People would tell us if you have two boys, so you are probably going to have a third boy. I immediately stood on Mark 11:24. Months later, we had Kelly, our beautiful baby girl. When you say you are going to stand on the word of God, you have to stand. You cannot let anyone's voice outweigh what the word of God says.

I mentioned earlier Bishop would push you to excellence. I remember teaching my first bible study. By nature, I love to talk, and I can talk to anybody but on that night, I was a nervous wreck. When I got up to teach, I read straight from the bible. I would not even look at the people. When I was done, I was thought he is would be disappointed and tell me I had done a terrible job. Instead, he looked at me and said "Hutton-good job". He showed me then the process is just as important as the destination. He believed in me. This belief made me want to get better, so I began to read to increase my knowledge.

The first book Bishop gave me was called *The Day that Christ Died* by Jim Bishop which summarized the last hours of Jesus. Once I read this book, I started to understand how much Christ loved me and why he would die for me. (John 3:16 *"For God so loved the world, that he gave his only begotten son, that whosoever believeth in him should not perish, but have everlasting life"*) I studied the word of God and understand the customs of the day in order to understand the context of what I was learning. I read more and more. The second book Bishop gave me was *The Tongue: A Creative Force* by Charles Capps which talks about the importance of what you say. Both of these books helped me better understand what this Christian walk should look like.

Earlier I stated, I was a talker by nature but after reading the book on the tongue, I realized I needed to watch what I say to others and how my words have power (Proverbs 18:21 *"Death and life are in the power of the tongue: and they that love it shall eat the fruit thereof"*). I now began to understand how much Christ loves me and the importance of watching what I say. However, I still did not know how to serve.

Remember I said I felt God was grooming me for something, though I was not quite sure what it was. I started to realize it when I read a book on Servanthood. I was going to serve the man of God and the three things I needed to learn quickly was Christ loved me, watch what I say and how I say it and how to serve. I went all in on this thing. Having come from a military background, one of the rules we lived by was protect yourself and protect those around you. As a servant of the Lord, I was always going to serve Bishop with everything I had in me and protect him at all cost.

There was a time when we were on Balboa Street in Greensboro, North Carolina. This was the first church we were in. I wanted to use one of the rooms and move in so I could be available to the ministry 24 hours a day. Bishop told me no. He said I could not do that because I needed to have balance between the ministry and my family. He later told me "Hutton, there are no more of you out there. Your commitment is supernatural". This was one of his greatest compliments to me, but he always made sure I was there for my family. He always made sure I did not allow church responsibilities get in the way of being a husband and a father.

One of the things I loved about Bishop Lockett was he had a commanding presence, but he did not want you to always agree with him. I remember one day he said "Hutton, you try to avoid me getting on you, so you do exactly what I say to do and how I say to do it. You are not thinking outside of my instructions which meant you are not being creative." He wanted me to have his back. For Bishop, the best way to have his back was not just about following orders. He wanted leaders to respectfully challenge him if they felt a decision was not in the best interest of the people and the ministry. He wanted a leader who would think about all of the possibilities, both negative and positive. As his armor bearer, I was learning my role was not to serve blindly but protect him from any potential pitfalls he may not initially see.

I had the privilege to do this for over 35 years. Then on October 12th, 2012, my spiritual advisor, my bishop, and my friend transitioned from this earth to be with our Heavenly Father. He was only 58 years old when the Lord decided to call him home. He would often say to our church, "You may miss me, but don't miss my God". Little did I know I would have to rely on those words to get me through one of the toughest times of my life.

No one expected Bishop Lockett to pass. Evangel Fellowship and our friends in the ministry had all been praying and fasting. We believed God would heal him on this side of Glory. When he passed, we all felt the pain of grief. This was a huge loss to our church and to our community. Some people were upset they did not know what was going on and how sick Bishop was.

Unfortunately, several people close to Bishop found out from social media he had passed. The ministry's board of trustees consisting of Elder William Thompson, Elder Michael Lewis and I had to deal with that. I also felt the need to protect the family and their privacy. There were many times I found myself explaining to people, the family needed some time to grieve. It was necessary to respect them and allow them the time they needed to heal.

With everyone reeling from Bishop's passing, I had to deal with my own emotions and questions. Everyone always expects leadership to be strong. You are supposed to have all the answers and be there for everyone. I knew the people needed me and I knew Bishop would want me to be there for them as he had taught me. But I was going through my own set of questions and grief. Bishop held a special place in my heart and in my life. In Deuteronomy 34:8, it states when Moses died *"the children of Israel wept for Moses in the plains for Moab thirty days"*. I expected to be okay in a week; but I was not okay.

To be honest, I was upset with God. I felt like God had let us down. I wanted to break down, but I could not. The worst part was I did not feel like there was anyone I could share my feelings. We all were all dealing with the loss of our spiritual father. I was concerned about Sister Lockett and the kids. I did not know how I was going to deal with the death of my best friend and pastor.

I did not know how to keep everyone encouraged when I was feeling my own loss. My heart was so heavy. There were days I wondered if I would make it through the pain. It was gut wrenching. There were many days, my grief felt like it was consuming me. The questions kept coming to my mind. What will happen to the people of God? Where do I go from here God? What do you want me to do? There were so many questions and so few answers. I prayed but often felt numb. It was if a part of me had died with him.

One morning, about a month after Bishop had passed, I was laying in my bed feeling pretty down when I heard God speak. He asked me, "What did I tell you to do when you first started in the ministry?" I answered him "Go help Otis". He then asked me what did Otis tell you to do? I said, "Help his sons". It was at that moment I realized I needed to stop having a pity party. I needed to get up and go help, not only his spiritual sons in the ministry, but his biological sons. They had just lost their father and were now thrust into the roles of pastors and leaders. I knew I had to serve them like I had served Bishop.

Bishop often said, "Miss me but don't miss my God". Those profound words came back to me. I realized I would have to use the pain I was feeling as the fire pushing me to carry on the legacy this great man left. Bishop would often preach from James 1:2-4 *"Count it all joy when ye fall into divers' temptations; knowing this, that the trying of your faith worketh patience. But let patience have her perfect work, that ye may be perfect and entire, wanting no thing."* I came to realize no matter how the trial looked, or how I felt about it, I needed to maintain a spirit of joy.

Of course, I wanted my pastor and friend to still be here, but my response needed to be one pleasing to God and to Bishop Lockett's legacy. So, I fought. I fought against the negative voices in my head telling me to give up, telling me it was over. Instead, I began to look at the legacy he left behind and what part I could play to continue that incredible heritage. I sought the Lord for wisdom and followed the word in James 1:5 *"If any of you lack wisdom, let him ask of God, that giveth to all men liberally, and upbraideth not; and it shall be given him."* I needed divine insight on how to help our ministry and his sons, biological and spiritual, get through to the other side of this.

There were many things I learned as we went through this process of figuring out what to do when Bishop transitioned. However, there were four principles which stood out. **The first was to grieve, then celebrate.** We missed Bishop but we wanted to celebrate his life and his legacy, so we created the Legacy Room. This room is dedicated to the memory and accomplishments of Bishop Lockett. Some months after he had passed, we had a huge dedication service. We adorned the space with photos of family and friends, videos of his sermons and a bookstore highlighting the great accomplishments through his ministry.

He may be gone but we were going to make sure he was never forgotten. This was not a one-man effort. It took all of us coming together to honor and memorialize the achievements of this great man. Now, I began to realize it was not all on me. I did not have to rely on my own strengths. There were people around me. Each of them had gifts, had strengths and talents. Though different from me, we would continue to strengthen our ministry. Ephesians 4:16 says *"From whom the whole body fitly joined together and compacted by that which every joint supplieth, according to the effectual working in the measure of every part, maketh increase of the body unto the edifying of itself in love"*. We would get through this and we would get through it together.

The second principle I learned was we needed to keep our ministry strong and prepare the people for change. One of the remarkable things about Bishop Lockett was his ability to plan. He was a planner. He had already spoken to Bishop Charles Blake, the Presiding Bishop of the Church of God in Christ, Inc. regarding his desires for his son, Pastor Otis Lockett, Jr. to take over the ministry of Evangel Fellowship. There was never any questions on who would replace Bishop as pastor of Evangel Fellowship. Additionally, he had lent his support and recommendation for Bishop Stenneth E. Powell, Sr., the current Jurisdictional Prelate of the North Carolina 2nd Ecclesiastical Jurisdiction.

Bishop Lockett's incredible pre-planning made things go smoothly for our church body. We were able to avoid some of the chaos many churches may experience when it is not clear who takes over after the loss of the pastor. One of his initiatives, prior to his passing, was to break up the district and appoint superintendents over each area. Roles were clearly defined and understood by all. While there were some hiccups along the way, much chaos was alleviated because of Bishop Lockett's visionary leadership.

One of the most disheartening things I experienced was seeing people break off into other districts outside of the 2nd Ecclesiastical Jurisdiction. However, one day I was thinking about the four men who wrote the four gospels. I thought to myself, God never tried to control them. He allowed them to use their own literary styles and observations, while writing their own accounts of the life of Jesus. I realized these pastors were fine men of God and they each had to follow what they felt was best for them. This helped me quickly get over my disappointments.

The third principle I learned was to support new leadership. I spoke earlier of a conversation with Bishop Lockett where he told me to take care of his sons. He meant his biological sons as well as his spiritual sons. When Pastor Otis Lockett, Jr. was first appointed to the ministry, I knew my calling was to serve the new man of God as I had served his father. I started by telling him things he may not have known regarding the business side of the ministry.

I shared with him everything I knew. Pastor O was easy to serve because he, like his father loved the Lord, had the same standards as his father and we all believed the same thing regarding the Word of God. In the beginning of his ministry at Evangel, people would often come to me or the other two Elders. We always redirected them back to Pastor O so they would see him as the leader of our church. We knew there were people concerned Pastor O may not understand certain things because he was young and unmarried. However, people quickly came to realize he possessed wisdom, so they came to accept him. They saw the board of Trustees supported Pastor O. They began to hear his heart concerning the vision he had for Evangel Fellowship. Combined with his knowledge of the word of God, they began to see him as their Pastor and Leader.

I am honored to serve Pastor O as I did his father for 30 years. I have served Pastor O now for 8 years. While I miss my Bishop, Pastor and Friend, it is just as he desired for all of us in his ministry. I may miss him, but I do not miss his God because I have come to know God for myself. I get the privilege of serving his son and hearing the word echoed through his son, Pastor O's voice. I know God is in heaven saying to Bishop, *"Well done thou good and faithful servant: thou hast been faithful over a few things, I will make thee ruler over many things: enter thou into the joy of thy lord".* Matthew 25:21 KJV

ROGER HUTTON

Oxford defines a servant as one who performs duties for others; a devoted and helpful follower or support. The biblical definition of a servant is found in Peter 2:16 which describes servants of God being free to act within the bounds of God's will. Elder Roger Hutton has been honored to serve under both Bishop Otis Lockett, Sr. and Pastor Otis Lockett, Jr. for 38 years.

Elder Hutton also serves as Chairperson for the Elders, General Manager of Facilities and Head of Security for Evangel Fellowship Church of God in Christin located in Greensboro, North Carolina. Outside of being married to his wonderful wife Annette and having two great sons, one of my proudest moments are the birth of my daughter Kelly. His second proudest moment was when his son Roger Hutton, Jr. and his wife Cynthia gave their lives to Christ and my son began serving in the ministry.

If Elder Hutton had to give anyone advice about serving in the ministry, it would be to make sure you count the cost. Make sure you discuss it with your spouse, and you are both in agreement regarding the commitment and time it will take. Serving is not an easy task and it is not for the faint of heart. We were in total agreement on what this meant and the sacrifices necessary regarding our family. Elder Roger Hutton can say without any doubt it has been one of the most rewarding experiences in his life. He is honored God has chosen him to be one of his servants.

REFLECTION

Serving Through The Death of My Pastor
"This trial might not make sense, but it will make faith."

Let's be honest. Many of us are confused, wondering, and downright mystified by the way God has operated in our lives. We have questions. I have questions. And, the truth be told, we often say, "We'll understand it better by and by", as a cover-up for how we really feel. God, why? God, really? God, what for? God, how could you? We use the standard answers like "It will be alright", to help us navigate the painful, heartbreaking, moments we face on this life's journey.

When my Pastor died, Bishop Otis Lockett, Sr., I admit I was beyond perplexed. Not because I did not believe God or believe His Word. But I could not understand His timing. Bishop Lockett was not old, or incapacitated. He was full of vision and purpose. He was ready to see God's promises and plans come to fruition. He was focused and looking forward to the next move of God in the earth.

What I came to realize was, even in death, he was still teaching me how important faith for him and for us. He left for me, the example of believing God, faith in God, no matter what. Though he fought to stay, he ultimately submitted to God's timing and God's will for Him. He still believed purpose would be fulfilled through those who would come after him. Even in death, he believed God.

- Grieve, but whatever you do, do not give up on God. It is painful but your faith is not in the person. Your faith is in God.

- Believe what your leader believed. Stay committed to the vision.

- Honor their life through yours. People will know who you served by who you are.

PART THREE:

THE PART LEFT OUT

13

"The Reason I Didn't Quit"

Odell Dickerson, Jr.
Chief Operating Officer | New Psalmist Baptist Church
Baltimore, MD

Whenever you embark on something new, a goal, job, relationship, or project, your mentality is set to see it through to completion. You never start something with the intention to quit before it is finished. You will encounter some things along the way and rarely do you believe those encounters will take you off course. While you may have calculated some risks and obstacles you believe are unavoidable, those calculations never catch all of the scenarios you are destined to encounter.

It is when the inevitability of tests, trials and turmoil rise in your journey, you begin to examine your "why". Why am I here? Why am I doing this? Why is this important to me? Those and so many more thoughts challenging your decision to conquer this expedition arise. When you have tangible outcomes or rewards, it is easier to define those queries. If you are a new wife or husband, your "why" would be related to the love you have for your mate. If you are a new parent, your frustrated yet delighted response to lack of sleep and late night feedings is gladly accepting the responsibility of a new bundle of joy who is loved and wanted. When you are positioning yourself to buy a house and the overtime opportunities become a little taxing, you push through them because your 'why' supersedes the stress. Moments when we do not have a tangible result; when there is only an imaginary badge of honor, makes defining your reason for the action difficult.

We hear old adages like: *"Winners never quit, and quitters never win."* (Vince Lombardi), *"Never give up…"* (Winston Churchill), *"Quitting is not an option."* (Thomas Edison), *"Failing is not the worst thing in the world; quitting is."* (Edwin Louis Cole) or "*If you quit once it becomes a habit. Never quit.*" (Michael Jordan). They resonate well with us. They are really great and profound. They are encouraging and motivating. However, as good as they sound, they do not satisfy the feeling when your gut says, "This is not worth it." Those philosophical sayings do not speak to your core when you are wrestling with the pros and cons of what currently is and what could be if you just let it go or walked away.

THE BACKGROUND

In the spiritual world, our reasoning tends to be connected to our belief in our selected higher power and what we expect will result from our faith declaration. As Christians, we have heard, more times than we can count, Colossians 3:23, 24 *"Whatever you do, work at it with all your heart, as working for the Lord, not for human masters,"* *"since you know that you will receive an inheritance from the Lord as a reward. It is the Lord Christ you are serving."* It sounds so rich and rewarding. And it is.

However, ministry service, especially for adjutants and armor bearers, tests this scriptural reference on an unparalleled level. Being in someone else's life close enough to see their dirty laundry, literally and figuratively, is not for the faint of heart. This position requires you to carry extra baggage, in addition to your own personal load. So, while you are carrying those bags, filtering through the clothes, separating the delicates, the heavily stained and the soiled, you wonder how is not quitting' supposed to work? How is serving for the Lord and not for man, the man who may not respectfully consider your personal life or goals, really supposed to happen?

When everything inside your four walls, whether at home or occupationally, is pulling and tugging on you; and at the times when the loads of armor bearing laundry are the heaviest, how are you supposed to keep going? It is in the times when the challenges are chronic, the struggles are scurrilous, and the responsibility is rankling, one has to know, unequivocally, why you are doing the very thing exposing you to such adversity.

Although I am in no way a master at perseverance, I am mastering a perspective which best enables me to not quit. Why perspective, you ask? In my twenty years serving, from assistant to Chief Operations Officer, it has been proven my perspective is the primary thing that continued to push me forward. Let me take a moment and expound on perspective so you can understand my reason for not quitting.

WHAT IS PERPSECTIVE?

Perspective is defined by Merriam-Webster as mental view, prospect, or the capacity to view things in their true relations or relative importance. As a Christian, perspective is all locked into the relationship you have with God; and how sound and stable your relationship it is. Growing in God, which is a daily task, is what shapes your perspective. It enables you to see things as He sees them. Seeing life from God's view opens your world to a sundry of perspectives our carnal eyes could never see.

It sounds cliché however; it is the most liberating thing you can do in armor bearer or adjutant service. I am a husband, father of three and a full time Executive. In addition to the direct assistance, I provide my pastor in his travels, I had to learn, through the years, how to view things in their relative importance. Conversations with my leader to understand his expectations and my family to understand their needs was critical as well as each of them understanding mine, with the outside responsibilities I manage. I also had to introspectively dissect myself to know what I wanted so I could see how this area of service fit into the puzzle.

The only way the plethora of expectations can work harmoniously is with God. He knows me. He knows my leader. He knows my wife, my sons, and my daughter. Therefore, God is the only one who can bring it all into right perspective, so the pieces fit and fit correctly. Now having His perspective does not erase the emotional, mental, and physical toil I endured over time. Nor does it eradicate those elements of others involved. We have to make a conscious decision daily to not let our humanistic tendencies overwhelm us and override the grace we have been rationed for the day. It is a constant battle. And it can only be won with intentionality.

You have to deliberately decide you will accept God's guidance through the perspective He gives you and let it be what orchestrates your movements. After all, we are mainly contested with quitting when our world appears tough. We struggle with quitting when we think we are crashing or when a void has been identified.

What kind of clear perspective can you have when your vision is fogged by helplessness and hope-lessness? How can you determine what move is the best move if all you can see is nowhere to move? When the fog of frustration and the shadow of stress hovers over you, the responsibility of the armor bearer, adjutant or leadership role yet remains. And at times, the fog seems heavier when your pastor or leader adds to the frustration and stress in your life. Nevertheless, you are expected to provide fail-safe coverage and execute in excellence. Having the right perspective gives you enough sight and strength to keep you from being blind and bound in serving. Your perspective allows you to persevere to completion.

ESTABLISH YOUR PERSPECTIVE

Becoming a husband and father are two of the most rewarding roles I have assumed in my life thus far. The weight of those obligations has stretched me in ways I never thought possible. Because I hold my relationship with God in high standard, it is my mission to pattern my actions after Jesus and reflect his unwavering display of love. This is what has charged my perseverance to progress forward in all other capacities.

My family is what shapes my perspective. Every move I make affects them; directly or indirectly, whether I am with them or not with them and regardless, if they see or do not see me. My love for them is paramount and will not allow me to falter from excellence, endurance, and empowerment. Excellence because they have to know being outstanding or extremely good is always an achievable option. Endurance because they have to know they can make it through anything. Empowerment because they have to know being confident and strong gives them the control they need in living life.

The best way for me to teach these values to my two sons and daughter is through demonstration. It is a customary practice to adore and advise them as they grow into their own personalities. However, those words are like vapors without actions to validate them. Therefore, I take every chance to perform the principles I earnestly hope they will employ when faced with similar situations. Each individual has to take an introspective look and determine what one element will keep you on your chartered course until you have successfully conquered all it brings you.

While my motivation was packaged in the form of my offspring, yours may be completely different. Loving family and not disappointing them may seem like a general concept everybody can embrace, with or without children. However, it is your personal journey and all you have experienced makes whatever your determined outlook unique. No person wants to see their family, children, spouse, parent or otherwise suffer and go lacking. We all want to have our loved ones on earth with us as long as possible, enjoying the best life has to offer while they live.

Of course, we understand God has determined our destiny before our birth so we do what we can to maximize all we can in our undisclosed life span. For me, the course of my life before having children impacted me in a such a way it established the mindset I now possess as a father. My core values in fatherhood are actually applicable to the other positions I occupy. It is my conviction the established standards from your motivating vantage point, no matter what it is, will flood the other components of your life. This is guaranteed to happen when you rest in your relationship with God simply because He is the master of bringing everything together and doing it so well.

MAINTAINING YOUR PERSPECTIVE

Once you have determined your inspiration to persevere, it is imperative you identify the essences of it enabling your focus and energy, 'No' matter where required, to be unshaken. With my family, specifically my offspring as the influencers of my operating angle, my personal ethics were determined by the legacy I wanted to establish for them as well as the legacy I wanted them to create for themselves. From October 26, 2000 to January 25, 2006 when Odell, III, Jalen and Caleb entered my world, I locked into my legacy on a deeper wavelength.

Everything focused on how my descendants would be impacted by my decisions. In order for my integrity to remain solid, I had to be 'the' man no matter where I was serving. The man who extends a helping hand even when my arm is too weak to raise. The man who does not blow up when chaos circles me and challenges my sanity. The man who is fully present in every moment. The man who honors his leader and respects his assignment rather than forfeiting my assignment. The man who speaks life into the vision of my shepherd through the labor of my hands and the words of my mouth. The man who stands for right without mutilating what is wrong. The man who chooses the soft answer instead of inciting anger. The man who does not accept defeat as the final outcome. The man who does not quit.

The way I can apply those ethical characteristics in my support service to my pastor is consistently reminding myself I want my children to see AND do the same. With them at the heart of my perspective, I equate each move, each decision as I am making it for them. Although they may never know the internal elements of what my armor bearer or executive assistant duties entailed, my actions in service and leadership will be a part of my legacy.

It is a legacy that leaves a footprint on their lives. This footprint is a guide displaying why you do what you do, how to handle what you do, when to do what you do, when 'not to do what you do and, most importantly for me, for whom you do what you do. My service method-ology is the blueprint for their own creative legacy.

Aligning your outlook with God's view gives you the greatest ability to uphold what you have decreed is your reason, your standpoint, and your perspective. This variable will permit you to keep the main thing, the main thing. I do not have to wrestle with prioritizing because every step taken is grounded in my perspective.

The times where my efforts fell short or were questionable was when I was out of whack with my personal devotion. As a result, I did not hear God's voice and direction. Personal devotion and prayer time is critical to being endowed with strength and grace for each assignment. Personal devotion and prayer time is also the key to having clarity in thoughts, decisions, and actions. I cannot say it enough; God does all things well and is concerned about everything that concerns you.

PERSPECTIVE AND PROGRESSION

Now that you understand my why, rather what has me locked in the land of non-quitters, let me share one last thing. Establishing your perspective gives you the line of sight you need to not falter or fumble into failure. I would not do you any justice if I did not say even if your perspective does not change, the elements surrounding it will. Therefore, you have to learn how to be progressive in your perspective. My children entered the world as infants and have now developed into young men and women. With their growth came my growth. Growth in my leadership. Growth in my ministerial management. Growth in my overall service.

Yet, the challenges did not disappear. They merely camouflaged themselves as new people, new places, and new plots. Therefore, my family remained the charge of my commitment, while my foundational assignment to my leader also stayed the same. Meanwhile, I could not continue as the same Odell. I had to evolve. The Odell who accepted the assignment twenty years ago cannot be the same man today. It would mean I would not be as wise, experienced, or capable enough to be a champion in service and leadership. I would be foolish to expect my children, in toddler form, to be the amazing high school and college students they are currently.

Progression is vital to performing at your maximum level. That is why I continued to push and press. Fight and not fumble. Attack and achieve. Otherwise, I would have not been competent or classified to walk in the calling. The roots of a tree never change even though the tree goes through changes. Each season brings a new occurrence and enhancement. Being rooted in my perspective gave me the foundation I needed to remain planted in purpose while adjusting to the seasons.

Yes, there were, are and will be cold and freezing temperatures. There will be times when it feels like you are alone with no coat of courage or scarf of security and it seems you are freezing with frustration. Yes there were, are and will be rain and storms. Times when you have no poncho of passion or umbrella of understanding and it seems you are drowning in distress. Yes, there were, are and will be scorching rays of stress disguised as sunshine and it seems you are overheating from obstacles.

It is in these times you have two choices. These choices are two phrases made up of two words that qualify your perspective and your state of progression therein. Give up or don't quit. You may uncommonly hear someone tell you to give up. On the other hand, everyone will readily utter "don't quit." My perspective, my family, has taught me to uniquely merge the two statements. Give up what does not apply and do not quit what matters. What matters lies in your perspective...what empowers your focus and commitment. Consequently, everything that does not apply is released. Consider your favored superhero and villain story. Each had a path which brought them to the crossroad of consciousness...to embrace the powerful enhancement for good or for evil. Upon making the decision, the outcome was one choosing not to quit on the positive and promising side of humanity and the other quitting on it. It is safe to say their perspective on humanity was, whether it was worth saving or savaging. Does your perspective qualify you as a superhero or villain of service?

Take a minute to write down the top three things shaping your perspective. Next, ask yourself if those items implore you to give up or don't quit. If giving up is where you are, look at what encourages you not to quit. Now everything that works against your inspiration; everything that does not galvanize you to accomplish goals or authorize your total ability to be used in your assignment is what you give up. In a nutshell, this is the reason I did not quit. It is my hope you have been enlightened, encouraged, and enabled through my synopsis. Be powerful and DON'T QUIT!

ODELL DICKERSON

Odell Dickerson, Jr. serves as the Chief Operating Officer (COO) for New Psalmist Baptist Church in Baltimore, MD, where Bishop Walter Scott Thomas, Sr. is the Pastor. Currently, there are over 8,000 active members.

After becoming an official member of New Psalmist Baptist Church in May 1999, Odell became the Chief Operating Officer in June 2000. He also serves as Chief of Staff for the Ministry, Operation and Business Office staff. Additionally, Odell oversees the Office of the Bishop, which includes, but is not limited to, the operating functions of Bishop Thomas' office as both Bishop and Pastor.

He brings to ministry 20 years of experience serving at New Psalmist, as well as a bachelor's degree in Accounting and a master's degree in Business Administration. Outside of his many roles at New Psalmist, Odell consults for his own LLC, Odellexec Enterprises, and Changes Can Happen, LLC. His mission and passion are to strengthen organizations both secular and religious in leadership, culture, vision and mission implementation, financial wellness, and organizational infrastructure.

He is a devoted family man He is married to Sherri Dickerson and they are raising three beautiful children, Odell III, Jalen DeAnn, and Caleb James.

REFLECTION

The Reason I Did Not Quit

"One of the greatest motivations in ministry is your family, your faith, your name, and your example."

The honor I have being trusted with my children floors me every time I think about it. When they both came into this world, I was a clueless young father. I know my responsibility was to raise them. My job was to assist them in discovering their individual purpose and direction in life. The experience, in essence, "raised" me. I realized I could only teach them how to be, by being the example they needed.

I quickly had to rid myself of selfish ambition and make my drive inclusive of what was BEST for them. What was best for them was to not just hear me, but to see me. They needed to see me be driven, see me serving, see me compassionate, see me faithful, see me successful and see me trusting God.

There's never a day, I am not mindful of the beautiful woman that went to death's door in childbirth, to bring them to me. I'm called by a lot of titles these days, some I like and some I don't; but nothing makes me perk up like hearing "Dad" from my children, Efrim and Hope.

- Seeing your family is the moment when you are arrested by God, overwhelmed by purpose, and introduced to the reason why failure is not an option.

- Hebrews 11:7 NLT says, "It was by faith that Noah built a large boat to save his family from the flood." This father was intentional about saving his house and ended up saving the world. Invest in your family. It will not go unrewarded.

14

Adjusting To My Leader's 'No'

Reverend Dr. Alan P. Walker
Secretary-General | Greater Highway
Deliverance Ministries Inc. Manhattan, NY

Hebrews 13:17 Amplified Bible. *[17] Obey your [spiritual] leaders and submit to them [recognizing their authority over you], for they are keeping watch over your souls and continually guarding your spiritual welfare as those who will give an account [of their stewardship of you]. Let them do this with joy and not with grief and groans, for this would be of 'No' benefit to you.*

I am the Very Reverend Alan Patrice Walker, D. Min. and I serve as the Secretary-General of the Greater Highway Deliverance Ministries Inc., headquartered in Manhattan, NY. The Presiding Prelate of this fellowship of Churches is his Grace, the Most Reverend Liston Page Sr. and there are two Vice-Presiding Bishop's whose names are the Honorable Right Reverend Gerald Oden and the Honorable Right Reverend Liston Page II, D. Min. I have been a part of this fellowship since May of 2003.

It was my wife, Alicia Vanessa who had insisted we visit The Highway Church located in Paterson, NJ. At that time Bishop Liston Page II, (known then as Elder Page) was Pastor. He had not been consecrated as a Bishop in the Lords Church. My wife and I enjoyed the praise and worship as well as the expositional and insightful preaching of this young and energetic preacher. After having visited the church on several occasions, we decided to join the ministry and see where we could be used by God in this particular vineyard.

After attending the Highway Church for a few months, I was asked by Pastor Page to work with the administration of his personal itinerant ministry. At the time, I was currently working in a corporate environment. I agreed to volunteer my time and learn the ins and outs of working with other ministries outside of the Highway Church. These were ministries who had invited Pastor Page to come and share his religious and spiritual oratory gifting with their congregations.

As time had passed, I became very efficient in my assignment. My due diligence resulted in receiving the title of Administrative Assistant to the Pastor. Pastor Page is a successful itinerate speaker and is continuously sort after. I found myself travelling along with him and his musician (Pastor Jeffery Lamont White), a tremendously gifted and talented singer and organist. As time progressed, we travelled around the United States and abroad to various conferences and ministries. I would witness the power of God falling in a miraculous way in many meetings. I was privileged to see lives of many individuals transformed by the preaching of the unadulterated Word of God.

Now mind you, I was doing all of this while working full-time as a manager at a major telecommunications corporation Monday thru Friday. It became very tedious trying to juggle corporate and church responsibilities. Unfortunately, there were times when I did not come up to par on either task. I found myself putting too much time in one aspect and neglecting the other. In November 2007, I was faced with the challenge of a Reduction in Force (RIF) at my corporate job. I had to decide whether or not to seek a different position at the company or trust God and accept the offer from Bishop

Liston Page II to work at the local church in Paterson, NJ. So, in January 2008, I decided to work full-time in ministry.

Once I decided to leave the corporate world, life for my wife and I changed. I quickly realized there is a stark difference being full-time in the church as oppose to being in a corporate setting. The mode of operation is totally different. You no longer have the resources once enjoyed because they are no longer available to you. I began to see ministry totally different. As a full-time employee of the church, I no longer had the team of people I once relied upon to get tasks completed. I was the team. Church ministry has a way of humbling a person, especially when there is more task than people, complete with deadlines for assignments and tasks. Those are the days when you wish you had not made the decision to leave the comforts and convenience of corporate American.

Let's fast-forward in time. I now have been in this position for several years. I observed several of my colleagues being called to churches as pastors. I began to wonder why I had not been considered for a pastoral assignment or why it seems my ministerial ascension was stagnant and at a standstill. I began to feel very perturbed. It seemed many of my peers where being promoted to pastoral assignments or being consecrated into the bishopric. Needless to say, I began to allow baseless assumptions to take prominence in my mind. I wondered if God had forgotten me.

I have always been mindful of the scripture Luke 16:11 which states, *"And if you have not been faithful in the use of that [earthly wealth] which belongs to another [whether God or man, and of which you are a trustee], who will give you that which is your own?"* I thought I had met the qualifications of this text. Here I was, working in the vineyard of another man's ministry and caring for it as though it was my own. I was operating out of the assumption soon I would have been called in the office and told I had been chosen for a pastoral assignment. Well, that moment never came to fruition. So, I just settled on saying it was not for me at this time.

One day, while I was working at the church in Paterson, Bishop Page II asked me to come into his office to speak with him. When I came into his office, I began to wonder why he had called me in. Could it be I had forgotten or missed something? It turned out he wanted to speak to me about a Church in Toledo, Ohio searching for a pastor. Their current pastor was leaving the ministry and had no desire to pastor any longer.

Now mind you, I did not think anything about the conversation. I thought he was only mentioning it to me because the pastor was someone person we both knew. So, I was taken aback when he said to me, "I think you should submit your resume to the search committee of this particular church". I looked at Pastor Page in amazement. Was this some kind of joke or trick? To my surprise he was quite serious. He encouraged me to prepare my resume and send it in.

The Search Committee received my paperwork and asked me to come to a face-to-face interview in Toledo, Ohio. I was eager but yet afraid. Here, I am in a position of fright because I had no idea what I was walking into. Yet, this is something I was looking for. And I felt overlooked because I had never been offered an opportunity for a pastoral appointment, while others had. I attended the interview and was told by the committee I interviewed well. They indicated they would get back to me with further instructions regarding next steps in the process.

It turned out, I did not get the pastorate because the current pastor decided he did not want to give up ministry and came back to his pulpit. Needless to say, I was a little upset after finding out the position was closed, and they were not looking for a pastor since he decided to stay.

After having been through the process of interviewing for the position of senior pastor, I began to think should I continue on this quest or just wait to see what happens next. I asked to meet with Pastor Page. I discussed what I experienced during the interview process. I also asked him did he feel I should continue the quest for a pastorate? The answer I received was 'No'.

He clearly stated, I should not continue to look for a pastorate at this time. I was quite puzzled and did not understand why he felt that way. He explained his reasoning. He allowed me the opportunity to attend the interview because he wanted me to get the experience of interviewing with a Pastoral Selection Committee. He further said, the reason he said 'No', at this time, was because there is more training I specifically needed. This training was important to have before he felt comfortable releasing me to pastor.

At the time, I did not understand his 'No'. I felt I was ready. I just knew I had all of the necessary skills and could meet the challenge. Unknown to me, he had been grooming me for the eventual day I would leave the ministry and be called to a church. He explained to me he was not holding me back because he did not want me to leave. He wanted me to be fully prepared spiritually and academically. He stated, "I know what you are capable of and I see where God is taking you. But it is my job as your leader to ensure you have been trained and provided the education necessary to excel in the next level of leadership".

Here is the problem, I never went to my pastor to discuss my future. I just assumed I was going to be placed in a church because of my loyalty to the ministry and my connection to pastor as his administrator. My assumption was wrong and nearly cost me the relationship I had with my pastor and church. By having a conversation with my Man of God, I was able to understand why I was still operating on the same level. I was not ready for the next level or phase of ministry.

The results of my conversation with my Pastor motived me to go back to school. I not only got one degree but three degrees in total. Speaking to my leader, opened the door for an honest conversation. He explained to me my strengths and weaknesses, something all great leaders should do for their subordinates.

I had to adjust to my leader's 'No' because I did not clearly understand the plan God for my life. It is the responsibility of the leader to decipher what the Lord is doing in lives of those who follow them. Men and women of God, who are assigned to sit under a leader, must understand they are God's mouthpiece for our lives. We must conform to what they advise us to do, even if we do not understand what their intentions are. We have to trust and believe they are operating out of the will of God and it will work out for our good.

Too many men and women miss the will of God because they did not adjust or accept the 'No' of their leaders. Out of anger or hurt, they decided to move on without the blessing of their leader. We have to understand it is God who gives the leader authority over our spiritual lives. We have to understand those lives are hinged upon us following godly leaders we have been placed under. Many mistakes would not have taken place if we just learn how to adjust to our leader's 'No' and understand he or she is only doing the will of God.

God has uniquely placed each of us under specific spiritual leaders who are to disciple and groom us on our paths of destiny. It is vitally important the communication between the leader and subordinate stay clear of hindrances which will dwarf your growth in

God. Get to know your leader. Walk close with your leader. There are lessons you can only master when you are close in proximity. Do not be afraid to speak with your leader and to communicate how you feel about any learning track. Express to your leader your desire in ministry and allow them to instruct and prepare you for the arduous journey.

A leader saying, 'No' is not the end of a situation. In fact, it can be the start of something new and exciting. We have to learn how to adjust to our leader 'No' and understand he/she knows you. God has shown you to them in visions and dreams. It is the desire of most leaders to see their subordinates exceed. It is a direct reflection on them and serves as a gauge letting them know their teaching is not in vain.

Understand the 'No' of the leader is not the end. It serves as the safeguard keeping you from going off the deep end and allows you to stay in the realm of safety. The 'No' of the leader provides you time to get yourself together. It allows you to do an in-depth analysis of your life while letting you work on the rough areas of your life.

If it were not for the 'No' coming from my leader, and my ability to adjust to it, I would not be serving today as the Secretary-General of an Apostolic Pentecostal Fellowship. I would not have gone to Samuel Proctor School of Theology at Virginia University and received a Master of Divinity degree. I would not have graduated from Drew Theological School and received the Master of Sacred Theology and the Doctor of Ministry degrees. I am grateful to my leader for saying 'No'. In the stage of 'No', I learned who I am and how to interact with my colleagues and peers. In the process of adjusting to the 'No', I learn how God is speaking to me through my leader and what the expectation God has for me.

I had to learn how to embrace the 'No' coming from the mouth of my leader and pray God's will for my life when my leader said "No, not now". Once my leader had spoken, it was up to me to receive it, find out why it was given and what lesson was intended. 'No' from the mouth of the leader is not a death sentence. It is only a temporary delay on the train tracks of your life.

Each time the leader says 'No', understand they are hearing from God and the purpose, behind the 'No', is to develop you into the best you can be. I am so glad my pastor said no. His 'No', prevented me from being something other than what God had said. And I certainly did not want to be out of the will of God. God has established leaders to care for His flock. We must adhere to what our leaders are saying in order for God to have full reign in our lives.

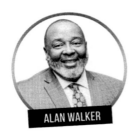

ALAN WALKER

Reverend Dr. Alan P. Walker was born in Brooklyn and raised in Georgia. The oldest of three, Dr. Walker was the first in his family to give his life to Jesus Christ at the age of 28. It wasn't too long after this life-changing decision where he not only found himself in service to the US Navy in 1979, but most importantly, in the army of the Lord where He has given His life as an offering over the past 25 years.

Dr. Walker was ordained an Elder at the National Holy Convocation of Greater Highway Deliverance Ministries per the choosing and confirmation of Bishop Liston Page II (Senior Pastor) in 2008. During his time as Pastoral Assistant and Elder, he was elevated to the office of Overseer by the Presiding Prelate of Greater Highway Deliverance Ministries, Inc., for the NJ Jurisdiction. And, in response to his acceptance of a call beyond the preaching ministry – the call into pastoral ministry, Dr. Walker accepted appointment to Administrative Pastor in 2010.

Reverend Dr. Alan P. Walker holds a Doctor of Ministry in Pastoral Care and a Master of Sacred Theology from Drew University. He also holds Master of Divinity in Religion and Theology from Samuel DeWitt Proctor School of Theology at Virginia Union University. He has been happily married to Alicia Vanessa Carter-Walker since December 21, 1990.

REFLECTION

Adjusting To My Leader's No

"You will not be successful if you will not take correction from a mentor that is bold enough to give it.'

God places authentic spiritual mentors in our lives to ensure we are operating in the will of God and not in our own selfish ambitions. Submission to real and reliable Godly leaders helps us to maintain our spiritual focus, protect our anointing, safeguard our God-ordered steps and care for our souls. Our God-appointed leaders often have the uncanny ability to discern our weaknesses and to predict our pitfalls. The thing we're trying to hide from them, they have seen many times before. We must learn to listen. We are trying to go where they have been. They have seen others who heeded the voice of the Lord, through them, and witnessed their supernatural success. And, they have watched the spiritual demise of those who saw their advice as a hinderance to their call.

I have had spiritual sons and daughters who have received "No" and those who have not. A "No" does not mean you are not anointed. It could simply mean you may not be ready, or the environment is not safe. A "No" is not a denial of elevation or promotion. There may be more work to be done, more self-development, more training, more education, or more meaningful relationships must be cultivated. Try to see "No" not as a rejection of you personally, but as an opportunity to learn, to be better prepared and to accomplish all God intends for you. 'No' paves the way for greater k**No**wledge, in**No**vative ministry, and an ho**No**rable service to the Lord.

- Your mentor has something you do not have because they know something you do not know. Be teachable.

15

Ardor Never Trumps Order!
Pastor Ishmael Wilson
Senior Pastor | Another Level Church
Capitol Heights, MD

When you think about what you want to become in life, you may typically start with areas that you admire or skills that you enjoy. At a very young age, I was attracted to karate. I watched every karate movie out in the 80's. From "The Last Dragon" to the "Karate Kid." You could not tell me I was not "LEROYYYY!" One day I was watching another karate film and all of a sudden about 20 men with black karate suits and black mask came out with weapons like stars and swords. That is when it hit me I wanted to become a ninja. Some of you may be laughing right now but, after that moment of awe, I began to develop an affinity for martial arts.

I never officially went to a martial arts class or school, but I spent countless hours of binge watching martial arts films. I developed a *passion, an ardor* which birthed an aspiration to become what I was watching. The word ardor simply means enthusiasm or passion. Ardor (*Passion*) leads to the discovery of your promise, but promise is not respected or honored without process and order. These are two words not fully embraced in the church but are equally important to the development of the whole person.

Process means a series of actions or steps taken in order to achieve a particular end. Order means God's decided path to reaching a particular outcome or goal. When we as the Body of Christ learn how to respect them both we will get to our expected end. This is something I learned early in my walk with God.

At the age of 8 years old, I had an encounter with God. In that encounter, God spoke to me and told me I would preach the Word of God. Though this promise from God manifested many years later, I knew even at 8 years old the call of God on my life should not be viewed as a life prison sentence, but a privilege to serve and represent Jesus Christ in the earth. So, I went from being an Altar Boy in the African Methodist Episcopal Zion Church to a Deacon in the Lord's Church at the age of 19 years old. I was the youngest Deacon in the organization at the time. Some questioned my Pastor's decision, but I believe wholeheartedly God did this because He knew I understood process and order.

As ministers of the Gospel, especially young ministers, we find it hard to wait our turn. After hearing the call and accepting the call, we want to move right into what God had said. But that is not how this works. There is a process we must endure first. Nothing happens overnight. There must be a period of waiting initiated within us, so we have an appreciation for the gift of God being developed inside of us.

This gift was placed there before we were in our mother's womb. The Bible says in Jeremiah 1:5 *"Before I formed you in the womb I knew you, before you were born I set you apart; I appointed you as a prophet to the nations."* God affirms his call on Jeremiah's life by assuring him the call happened long before he actually heard it. Jeremiah's call happened at the beginning. Everything Jeremiah would become; he had already become in the mind of God. And much like Jeremiah, we too have already become what He has called us to be. It is our responsibility to walk out what He has already released in us. Our problem is we want to walk in what He said without process. This is a mistake I have seen too often.

Some think you receive the call from God, and you preach tomorrow. You cannot receive the call and fulfill the call at the same time. God spoke to me at 8 years old and told me I would preach His word. I was ordained a deacon at the age of 19. In that same year, I preached my first message and was licensed as a minister. One year later at 20 years old, God spoke to me again. He said, "One day you will pastor my people." Now what I did not reveal to you earlier was my training started before I preached. I was trained to carry the Word by carrying the Word. At the age of 16, I became my Pastor's armorbearer.

I remember the day he selected me to serve. He asked me to get his Bible from the pulpit after he finished preaching. I got his Bible and stood there while he greeted every visitor and member of the church. I knew then God was training me for something greater. I served my pastor every Sunday for 5 years. I was so committed to serving and driving my Pastor, I neglected purchasing the type of car I wanted. Why? Because I knew the type of car I wanted would not allow me to adequately serve my Pastor. Whenever he called, I served with gladness. I served with gladness from the moment I started until the day the church unfortunately folded.

I was without a church for almost 6 months, before I found the next place God wanted me to be planted. When I joined the next ministry, I was still called by God to pastor. Remember, God called me to preach at 8. I did not preach my first message until I was 19 years old. I was ordained a deacon, licensed as a minister. Now the church I loved was closing its doors forever. Traumatic is the word most appropriate for this kind of devastation. The man who was like a father to me, who I faithfully served, was closing the doors to the church he founded.

Fast forward to 2012. Here I am joining another church with all of this experience. However, after meeting with the Assistant Pastor, I was told I would be "Brother Ishmael" at this church. Literally, it meant all of my previous accomplishments were not even going to be acknowledged. Serving God and His church was more important than the titles I carried. Now, you must understand I have a sure word from the Lord. I will Pastor by the time I turn 28. Yet, this church God told me to join was not going to acknowledge my credentials. I was devasted. I was confused. I was unsure. I felt I had missed God. I was passionate about what I had been called by God to do. I was gifted to preach and to serve my man of God.

Somewhere in between my service to God and His Church, the spirit of pride had come in. This spirit had begun to overshadow the call because now I relied more on the gift rather than the purpose of the gift. So, God used my new church to establish me in the kingdom properly and not on gift alone. Humility has to become the primary attribute you acquire. If it is not, then the spirit of pride will make you think your Pastor's accolades are yours. You were placed there to under-gird, support, and serve your leader, not be served. When God selected you as an armorbearer or adjutant, he selected you to a position of privilege. You have been chosen to minister to your leader.

When I think about a biblical example of what this kind of ministry should look like; it would be Moses and Joshua. Joshua was loyal to Moses. Joshua was the epitome of what longevity in serving looks like. Joshua served Moses for forty years as his minister and confidant. Joshua was not looking for opportunities to be seen. He stayed hidden. If you want to know how to qualify for your next level, stay hidden. This is some-thing I always knew was critical to my success as a servant. I was humble. The scripture, in 1 Peter 5:6, says *"Humble yourself therefore, under God's mighty hand, that he may lift you up in due time (NIV)."*

Humility will elevate you faster than zeal. This is why Moses made Joshua apart of his succession plan. Joshua knew how to stay low and allow God to exalt him. Joshua endured the process. Joshua was there as Moses went through several stages of his own personal walk with God. What Joshua saw others were not privy too was never revealed. Joshua understood what it meant to be a confidant to his leader. I want to pause here and stress this point. As a servant leader, you are called to be your man or woman of God's confidant. You are a trusted voice on the team.

I can remember several situations I was privy to be with leaders I have served, but I have never spoken about them, because what you see should not be shared. Does your leader have weaknesses? Yes. Will you see things others will never see? Yes. Will you be privy to conversations that should never leave the room? Yes. You are their confidant. Confidants cover. They never expose. When Noah became drunk, after drinking the wine from his vineyard, he was laying in the tent uncovered. Ham, his son, saw him and went to tell his brothers, Shem, and Japheth. Shem and Japheth took a garment and draped it over their shoulders like a cape. They walked backwards towards their father so they could not see their father's nakedness and covered him. This is the position every servant leader must take.

If you are not willing to cover your leader in the good and the bad, then resign from your position. You are not only called when things are good. You are also called when things do not turn out the way you imagined. I know you thought every Sunday and Wednesday night would be glamourous. But real serving happens when the sanctuary is dim, and the people are gone.

I can remember days leaving the church early in the morning. After bible study, I packed product to prepare my leader for a week of ministry. I would leave the church after making sure the product, inventory list and credit card machine were all in the suitcase. Then, I would go to his house, and make sure his clothes were packed. I would bring it all back to the church meeting the driver who would take him to the airport by 4:30am for a 6am flight.

After I saw him off, I made sure the office was locked up and everything was properly stored. I would go home, shower and lay down for an hour or two only to get back up and work 9-hour shift. This is the part of ministry not discussed. Everyone wants to be close to their Pastor, but not everyone is willing to earn their position next to the man or woman of God. No matter how hard it may get, never forget the privilege it is to serve your leader. God only calls a few to stand with the Senior Leader. If you are one of them, then honor that call. You must handle it with the utmost integrity.

When I think about the idea of serving, I think about Jesus who was a servant leader. According to John Maxwell, "A servant leader is a leader whose focus is on serving others rather than being served." You can see throughout the scripture how Jesus served. Jesus even served while he was on the cross. According to Luke Chapter 23, he ministered to the thief hanging next to him. Because of Jesus' service on the cross, that thief accepted Christ as Lord and was assured a place in paradise. What a true embodiment of servitude. I have had my share of ups and downs as a servant in ministry and the marketplace. Yet, I know my life has been advanced and enhanced because I am a servant at heart. Serving is who I am and not something I "do."

Like I mentioned earlier in the chapter, I was licensed to preach when I came to one of the ministries I joined. However, my license was not even honored at the time. God wanted to make sure I was coming to serve the ministry and not use my gift to preach. There was something greater God wanted to birth in me pivotal to my development. There was an order I had to comply with. God wanted to test my character before He spotlighted my call. I can recall many instances of serving my Pastor at a time whom I often felt he did not like me. But, because I respected the God in him and his anointing, I continued to serve like I was his favorite.

God revealed to me through that season of ministry what He was doing in me was bigger than "personality flaws or gaps." I knew God was using him for my future while perfecting my now. The question for all who are currently serving is, "Are you willing to serve when things do not feel good, sound good, or look good? Are you truly willing to die to your flesh in order to fulfill your assignment from God?

Which brings me to another great point. It is understanding your assignment. When you understand your assignment, you do not allow your own personal goals or aspirations in ministry to cloud your full commitment to serve. It is vitality important to you and your leader you are clear about your call to him or her. When you are not clear about whether the person you are serving is part of your assignment, then serving will likely be challenging most of the time. If you are just serving to get something for yourself, you will likely experience regular challenges with serving. Many people in the body of Christ identify opportunities to serve based on where they feel God is taking them. They think to themselves, "I am called to preach so I will serve the Pastor." "I am called to lead adults, so I'll sign up for the first leadership opportunity presented." This is certainly a recipe for a disaster. You must serve according to your assignment and not because you desire something you have not been called to. You can get mentors to help build your capacity and grow you. Do not ever consider connecting with God's chosen leadership because you are thinking about your own personal advantage.

When you know serving is your assignment you do not stop and start when you want. An assignment will keep you serving even when you know they are disappointed in you, feel like they dislike you, or you are not their favorite. When you are serving out of assignment, you will be offense free. True assignments will present God ordained possibilities.

Because I allowed myself to be processed and served my leaders, God has entrusted me with more than I could have ever imagined. Today, I have a thriving church, a multi-site business in the DC Metropolitan area and a family who loves me. I know without a shadow of doubt things turned out like this because of the service rendered to every leader I served. I have been pastoring for over 12 years now. After 25 years of serving, I will still serve to this day.

Serving does not stop when you are now qualified to be served. I demonstrate for every leader in my church how to serve when my Bishop is around. I carry his Bible, order his food, pay for his meals, and drive him every opportunity I get. I am also the Chief Operating Officer for his personal ministry. Everything I did when I was just a minister trying to be accepted, I still do as an Overseer in the Lord's Church.

Titles do not stop your assignment. My assignment is a part of my destiny. Serving my leader never stopped being my assignment. I want every person who is reading this portion of my journey to know God sees every emotion you are feeling throughout your journey.

He knows every time you wanted to give up and you did not. He saw every tear you cried in silence. He was shaping you into the person you are right now. Whether you are just starting, or you have been serving as long as I, God sees all and He rewards faithfulness. Proverbs 28:20a says, *"A faithful man shall abound with blessings..."*

I know from experience what it is like to want to be used in ministry. I know what it is like when the protocol of the house puts parameters on how you are used. But, you have to stay the course. You cannot allow your zeal or passion to frustrate you while you are in the process. God is a God of order. And we must be a people who submit to order. It is written in Titus 1:5 *"The reason I left you in Crete was that you might put in order what was left unfinished and appoint elders in every town, as I directed you."*

God has chosen a man or a woman to establish order in his house. It is our responsibility as servant leaders to submit to that order and become who God has called you to be for His Glory. Remember my dear friends, ardor never trumps order because order is the will of God and ardor is your own will...*not my will but thine be done* (Matthew 6).

ISHMAEL WILLIAMS

Ishmael Wilson is a driven entrepreneur and pastor who is dedicated to empowering men and women. Ishmael Wilson often says, "Destiny doesn't happen without your participation", and that's what he has demonstrated for the world to witness. He is the founder and lead pastor of, Another Level Church (ALC) in Capitol Heights, Maryland and has served in this capacity since March 2, 2008. The church has grown tremendously over the past 12 years with an Administrative Office, an Empowerment Center, and Dry Cleaners. Ishmael Wilson holds a Bachelor of Arts in Leadership Development from Faith Christian University and Schools.

Annually, Pastor Ishmael host the Small Church Conference. In existence for four years, it is designed to empower "small church" pastors and leaders with tools and resources. His belief is, "Just because you're small, doesn't mean you can't be effective." Ishmael currently serves as the Chief   Operating Officer of the Donald Hilliard Ministries. Where he oversees all ministry business and philanthropic endeavors for the ministry.

In 2019, Ishmael opened up his fourth dry cleaner location. Fresh Dry Cleaners located in DC & MD. He is the proud co-founder of Success Geeks Inc, a brand that sets out to build the capacity of men and women in the areas of business, finance, career empowerment and personal development. Ishmael is also the proud author of two books entitled, "Prescriptions for Your Situation, Daily Doses for a Better You, which focuses on family, finance, faith, and love. His latest book release, is "10 Essential Keys: Building a Business That Outlast Any Crisis."

REFLECTION

Ardor Never Trumps Order

*"Having the energy for a race and knowing the route
are two totally different things."*

Zeal has never been something which alluded me. I love God, God's people, and I love serving. Serving ignites me, fuels me, and provokes me. What I had to learn in all of my enthusiasm, was to esteem God's voice, God's timing, and the ecclesiastical systems necessary for my maturation, my education, and my protection. There were moments I could not understand why I was not allowed to progress forward. I understand them now.

As a young preacher, committed and zealous, I was blessed with the opportunity to stand alongside renown Kingdom generals. Assigned with opening their preaching conferences with prayer and exhortation, I can recall a moment, I went out to exhort the audience. No one moved. I mean literally, no one moved. No one smiled, stood up, clapped, or even said Amen. Needless to say, I was a bit bewildered. I had put all of my vitality and vigor into my exhortation. I ministered with all the exuberance I could muster up. I gave it all I had.

After the event, I asked my mentor, what did I do wrong. The answer was simple. "Borders, you were prepared, you just were not ready." While my information was excellent, I had miscalculated who the people had come to see. They came to hear the voice of God through those designated to deliver it. It was not about me. Instead of listening to the Holy Spirit, I had mistaken my zeal as the catalyst for their response. The next night, when my assignment came, I stepped aside for the Holy Spirit. It was defining moment. This time, the response from the audience helped me understand who they came to see. They came to see God.

- You need both knowledge and wisdom. It is great to be tooled for success, but it is even better to know how to effectively use the tools you have been given.

16

I Didn't Sign Up For This

Nickolus South
Chief Adjutant |
Michigan Southwest First Jurisdiction COGIC
Detroit, Michigan

*"Not everyone can be an adjutant. There is a skill,
a presence, a grace. Adjutants represent the
organized, dignified display of heavenly worship
in the earth."*

For me, being an adjutant (a personal assistant to my pastor) has been an honor, a privilege, and a sacred trust. In my personal exploration and examination of the word commitment, it's rarely a question of facts; rather, it has been a question of my dedication and ability to remain focused. I am responsible for being an exemplar of this sage quote *"Being an adjutant is a presence, not a position."*

And with all that said; **"I DID NOT SIGN UP FOR THIS!"**

For most of us, if we are honest, we have to admit we are focused more on our desires, than our destiny. Desire is what we have requested from God, but destiny is what God is requiring from us. It is dangerous and potentially detrimental when what we want FROM God takes precedence over what God wants FOR us. **Every desire requires an equal depth of discipline.** I bring this to the conversation in the spirit of transparency. I share openly I have always desired to serve as an adjutant, to be a source of strength and consistent spiritual safety with and for my leaders. However, the demands placed on me, during 2020, were more intense than any other time in my life. They required a deeper determination and dedication than I knew I possessed. I will explain how and why a little later.

In church, many people are confused in their thinking. They believe proficiency in one area automatically qualifies them for promotion in another. Promotion is always a consequence of process. There are certain places in God you cannot desire your way into, rather you have to be disciplined into over a period of time and refined through experience. There are no pain killers and epidurals. There is no spiritual anesthesia.

In this highly technological age, those privileged to serve in senior servant ministry capacities (what I love to refer to as the "second chair") are often unknowingly anesthetized, losing their sensitivity and saliency. Social media has in many instances desensitized, misconstrued, and misrepresented the true essence of what this sacred calling is and what doing it effectively requires. As a result, if we are not careful, we have adjutants whose ideology of God, is not based on experience with God. Instagram provides snapshots, but it does not give a real picture of what it requires to serve sacrificially. Consequentially we have, in many cases, amassed an army of assassins, instead of a solemn and sanctified assembly of adjutants.

Having served as an adjutant, and preeminently as Chief Adjutant, let me humbly yet diaphanously share the function and focus of the Adjutancy is to be vicariously experienced. This experience is not conveyed mechanically through an unbroken chain of laying on of hands. It is expressed with continuity through the unbroken chain of commitment, beliefs and mission which started with the first biblical armor bearers and adjutants. Allow me, if you will, to share my revelation of who I am as an Adjutant. I do this, so conversely, you will understand and appreciate when I say, in spite of all I know, believe, and enjoy with regard to the Adjutancy,

"I DID NOT SIGN UP FOR THIS!"

"And the LORD spake unto Moses and Aaron, because ye believed me not, to sanctify me in the eyes of the children of Israel, therefore ye shall not bring this congregation into the land which I have given them." (Numbers 20:12)

The motto of the Adjutancy **"Sanctify the Leader in the eyes of the people"** is drawn from this scriptural reference. One of the first things I recognized in examining the unique relationship between Moses (first Chair) and Aaron (second Chair), is the decision to prohibit them from entering into the promised land was imputed and executed upon them equally. Understanding the magnitude of the responsibility of assisting the leader is one thing, but adequately evaluating the risk of being an adjutant is at the forefront of the text. For me, this passage spoke volumes with respect to how reverently and reflectively my assignment must be considered because I did not sign up to be evaluated on a scale parallel to the leader!

Lesson One: If you share in the accolades, expect to share in the accountability.
"And he shall be thy spokesman unto the people. And he shall be, even he shall be to thee instead of a mouth, and thou shalt be to him instead of God." **(Exodus 4:10-16)**

I have always embraced and enjoyed the servant ministry. In examining God's love and support of Moses (first Chair) it is obvious with intentionality and implicit purpose, the Lord assigns Aaron (second Chair) to assist him as an adjutant. God requires Aaron to fulfill the faithful execution of this assignment before he reveals and releases Aaron into his primary purpose and anointing as High Priest.

Lesson Two: The anointing to serve (High Priest) is always preceded by and connected to the assignment (adjutant). This assignment is to cover a "crack", a need or opportunity for development in the life of the leader. It was Moses' need as leader that created a necessity for Aaron's gift.

I did not sign up to be the chauffer, personal caretaker, travel companion, reservationist, receptionist, scheduler, logistics manager, vehicle service manager, friend of the family ambassador, pseudo chief of staff, event planner, memo drafter, email editor, communications expert, public relations director, financial bookkeeper, reminder, greeter, appointment setter, itinerary developer and facilitator, project manager, or a plethora of other functions asked of me. However, the ability to effectively fulfill and execute these assignments preceded my anointing. Through these tasks I was able to exercise influence and have meaningful impact as Chief Adjutant.

Having served for more than twenty years (in several local, regional, jurisdictional, and national arenas) as an adjutant, I have seen the nepotism, favoritism, and narcissism which often plagues first families, churches, and other ministries as a whole. I learned how to skillfully employ protocols which negate the need to manage personalities. While I did not sign up to learn these skills, they were apart of God's process in preparing me for promotion. Just as Aaron observed the highs and lows of Moses, as an adjutant, I have seen my leader at the zenith of his strength and in the valley of despair. Each perspective has helped me to learn as an adjutant my personal image must be invisible, but my impact is undeniable. I am committed to perfecting my invisible presence. My invisible presence must always take precedence over establishing my visible place.

"When appointed as Chief Adjutant, I quickly realized the test of my efficacy was never a question of my calling, but an evaluative revelation of my commitment."

Being Chief Adjutant affords me vast opportunities while requiring me to be directly accessible to the Prelate. The ecclesiastical jurisdiction I serve is comprised of nearly seventy – five churches which are organized into twenty – two districts. On a yearly basis, we host four large scale jurisdictional settings coupled with various regional events and other functions the Adjutancy directly facilitates and or supports. The range of ceremonial and civic services encompasses installations of pastors and elders, communion celebrations, as well as funerals for a multi-plicity of leaders across various levels of leadership. All of these events have their own unique structure, internal protocols, and procedures. Working with a wonderfully innovative leader who is publicly appreciative, celebrative, and receptive to the work of the adjutancy, has fostered a climate making serving he and his family a sheer joy.

Often individuals are immersed in a mentality of entitlement which resists protocol. They choose to prioritize their personal preferences. In this arena, this attitude makes change painful and, at times, leading change almost untenable. During my initial time serving as Chief Adjutant; I briefly attempted to manage the wide range of services, all of which are comprised of varying degrees of preparation and planning. I did this while attempting to integrate training in a culture of resistance and resentment. My resolve has always been the preservation of the presence and dignity of the Prelate, even in the face of opposition. If individuals are allowed to eclipse the institution, then it calls into question the consistency and stability of the church.

I began 2020 with a renewed sense of excitement and elation. One of the things I love most about the adjutancy is its invariability. This invariability embraces the sedentary, regimented, regulated, institutionalized yet inspirational approach which provides the framework for logistics, service, liturgy, and worship. As Chief Adjutant, I relish and revel in the spirit of order and polity guiding and governing the work I am graced and grateful to be responsible for.

I love the Lord of the work and the work of the Lord with insatiable passion. I was envisioning the worship services filled with pageantry and splendor, along with the ecclesiastical presence in all its regalia. The times of fellowship and fun had during conventions, convocations and conferences were all on the horizon; each of them representing a time of learning and leading, giving me a sense of fulfillment and purpose. Then came March 2020.

An outbreak occurred. An epidemic happened. A pandemic materialized. According to the World Health Organization, an outbreak is the occurrence of disease cases in excess of what is normally expected. Now, an epidemic is more than a normal number cases of an illness, specific health-related behavior or other health-related events in a community or region. Yet a pandemic is defined as the "worldwide spread" of a new disease.

The precious names of the people listed below represent the *"personal pandemic"* I experienced and endured in 2020. Each of them is someone I was related too, served, dignified, loved, touched, was touched by, worked with, or was connected to in some way; and tragically lost in 2020. Yes, many of them were lost to the infamous Corona Virus (COVID-19) and others to various illnesses. The tears staining my soul in this very moment will never be erased.

"I DID NOT SIGN UP FOR THIS!"

Bishop Philip Aquila Brooks II
Bishop Nathaniel Wyoming Wells
Bishop Ted Gera Thomas
Bishop Rance Lee Allen
Bishop Mark Henry Blade
Bishop Timothy Titus Scott
Bishop Beauford Terry
Bishop J. Delano Ellis
Auxiliary Bishop Willie James Campbell
Auxiliary Bishop Veodis Gaines
Auxiliary Bishop Robert L. Harris
Auxiliary Bishop Clarence Alfred Lewis III
Auxiliary Bishop Clarence Morton
Auxiliary Bishop Robert E. Smith Sr.
Administrative Assistant Kevelin B. Jones Sr.
Administrative Assistant Nick S. Edwards Jr.
Superintendent John Beverly
Superintendent Paul Hester Jr.
Superintendent Myron Lett
Superintendent Wilfred Matthews
Superintendent Leon McPherson
Pastor Steven Dunlap
Pastor Eddie L. Parrish
Pastor Paul M. Hogan II
Pastor Sam Knowlton
Pastor Steven Hansberry
Elder Freddie L. Brown II
Master Freddie L. Brown III

Elder Arthur & Mrs. Josephine Robinson
Mother Willie Mae Sheard
Supervisor Angela Hooks
Assistant Supervisor Alma Jean Clark
Mother Annis Lucille Dunlap
District Missionary Sarah Pyles
Mother Elizabeth Alexander
Mother Leila Clemons
Mother Bertha Durrett
Mother June Ginyard
Mother Minnie Head
Mother Lillie B. Hicks Hogan
Evangelist Janice Hogans
Mother Lois Juanita Johnson
Missionary Debra Lawrence – McClain
Missionary Rose Marie Rimson Brown
Mother Luella Turner
Mother Jessie Mae White
Sister Cynthia Gaudy
Sister Eloise Head Singleton
Sister Elaine Head
Sister Illene Hegler
Sister Theresa McCutchen
Sister Dortha Mae Pitts
Rebecca Lynn Worth
Deacon Emmett Hogan
Brother Charles J. Johnson II
Brother Aaron Walls
Mr. Robert Keith Clark Sr.
Mr. William Norman
Mr. Kelvin Wheeler

In March 2020, the world as I knew it would change forever. For the next six months, I dismissed my own plans, willingly left my home, changed the course of my personal and professional goals, and prioritized the preservation of the life of my Prelate. His life alone became the focal point of my existence. As a global presence, when he and his beautiful wife announced they both had contracted the COVID-19 Virus, we had no idea the toll it would take, the veracity it would strike with, and the utter destruction it would leave in its wake.

As Chief Adjutant, I was called upon to provide service in a way I could never have signed up for. Rather, it was a service I was called and consecrated to give. The hospitalization of the Prelate, the unbearable death of our beloved First Lady, the loss of several of my own family members, the barrage of sickness among our local church, calamity, despair, and death seemed to last for an eternity.

As Chief Adjutant, I was now tasked with monitoring critical information which had direct implications surrounding health care decisions. I provided daily personal care. I was present to service the needs of other pastors and leaders who were experiencing the death of their loved ones and members. And, I had to ensure memorial services were compliant with local and state governmental parameters.

The sixty names listed above represent a part of me. They were former pastors, friends, family members. I have worshipped with them for more than forty years. They were mentors, people who helped me during the darkest days of my life They helped put me through college and gave me my foundation. They were Mothers in Zion, co-workers, and sources of joy and laughter.

They were those I was able to lean and depend on and those who were able to lean and depend on me. They represent pastors I have preached and ministered for and friends I spent so many hours laughing with and loving on. They were members of my local church, jurisdiction, reformation, and city. They were neighbors and cousins.

In multiple instances there were losses of up to six persons from the same family. Death after death. Day after day. Day after day of helping families navigate the unchartered waters of burying loved ones in what seemed like obscurity and oblivion. Weeks turned into months of assisting with the day-to-day care of leadership while supporting the evolutionary needs of ministry. Those needs ranged from in person to online and virtual platforms, encompassing all of the "behind the scenes" work required to make them, their memorials, and their life celebrations polished and professional.

I had to learn how to migrate from our traditional rituals of transition for our loved ones, to facilitating "virtual funerals". Funerals which ordinarily would have been overflowing with hundreds, and in some cases thousands, of people were now reduced to groups of twenty–five! Now, add to this the responsibility of managing the emotional rollercoaster of notifying family members, life-long close friends, church members, and other officials they are not allowed to attend the funeral service or burial rites. Yes, there are limitations on how many people can be present at the gravesite.

The routine relief used to assist with the grieving process, in the loss of so many loved ones, had been denied us in the midst of this pandemic. The methods we employ to express emotions, to sustain our faith as we seek for the grace to accept what God has allowed, were diminished and in some cases, dissipated all together. The ceremonial rites used to pay homage, to acknowledge, celebrate, and salute our fallen soldiers were silenced. Flourishes were not given, flags were not furled, resplendent declarations of resolution replete with words of sympathy to heal the soul were mute.

I DID NOT SIGN UP FOR THIS!

Being Chief Adjutant during a pandemic is something I would never have signed up for. However, it is something I was destined to do. This ministry, this calling, this consecrated commitment is not something that can be taught, rather it is caught. I now understand as a spiritual repository, I was being poured into, prepared, positioned, empowered, and purified to fulfill this need. The needs of my leader created a necessity for the gift of the adjutancy. The pandemic has produced a panoramic view. I am seeing the fullness of the role and responsibility. The demand of the situation determines the degree of dedication necessary to protect the integrity of the officer and dignify the office. This is a Privilege. This is an Honor. This is a Sacred Trust.

NICKOLUS SOUTH

The life of Nic South is one that bears the indelible imprint of the master's hand. Elder South strives to exemplify a life representing the power and presence of the Savior. A lifelong member of the Church of God in Christ, he has had the opportunity and privilege to serve on multiple levels of the church, including his service as Chief Adjutant for the Michigan Southwest First Jurisdiction under the leadership of his pastor & Prelate, Bishop John H. Sheard.

He is a noted and sought-after speaker, mentor, trainer, workshop presenter and church administrator, with a proven record of efficacy and impact. Chief Adjutant South has authored numerous developmental strategic planning and implementation guides for effective service in servant leadership. Through innovative interactive "LeaderSHIFT" sessions, he has successfully engaged hundreds of servant leaders, empowering them as they strive to perfect their craft.

He has served as a classroom teacher, principal, and as assistant superintendent of schools. He is aggressively involved in multiple organizations and is now poised to begin his pursuit of an Executive Juris Doctorate degree. As a servant leader, he is committed to provoking God's presence through prayer, praise, and prophetic teaching. He is In Service. By Sacrifice. To Sanctify.

REFLECTION

"I Didn't Sign Up For This!"

*"When God wants to use your gift, He gives you a stage.
When He wants to use your life, He gives you a storm."*

God will put you in a situation so powerful, it makes you realize who you are capable of being and who He created you to be. There are so many moments in ministry I encountered that demanded a personal redefining of myself. There are instants where you say to yourself, "How does God expect me to handle this?", or "Why does God expect me to handle this?" In the Voice Translation of the Word, God tells Jeremiah, in chapter 1, verse 5 this:

*"Before I even formed you in your mother's womb, I knew
all about you. Before you drew your first breath, I had
already chosen you to be My prophet to speak
My word to the nations."*

When I finally got the revelation of this statement from God, it was life changing. The redefining of myself had to be completed not through the lens of "me", but through the "eyes" of God. I had to recognize everything I deal or dealt with was orchestrated by Him. While I may see myself great, God sees me greater. Though I may see myself confident in my gift, God sees me confident in Him. In those spaces, where I feel overwhelmed and underdeveloped, I understand prior to me breathing, God authorized and empowered me. There is nothing I will encounter, confront, or face, God has not already equipped me to handle, no matter what it is.

- I am thankful for my struggle because without I would have not stumbled upon my strength.

- I learned early on that being "anointed for it" and "ready for it" are two totally different things.

17
Young But Not Dumb

Justin Marshall
Executive Assistant Pastor |
Christ Cathedral of the Triad | Greensboro, NC

Are we really ready for the next generation of leaders to lead or is it just something we say to appear to be forward thinkers? As a millennial servant leader and PK (preacher's kid), there are many things attached to my generation. Apparently, being too young and inexperienced is one. When we look at the idea and concept of succession, it sounds good to the untrained. But it is much more difficult to implement and even tedious to accomplish when we believe our successors lack the experience others claim to have mastered. There are a few things our emerging leaders should consider. There are also things our predecessors should convey if they plan to help grow this next group of servant leaders. Let me talk to us, millennials first.

Your maturation as a servant-leader should be influential to others. Your service should carry the weight of passion that pushes others lacking passion to be infused and enlightened. What you will discover in your ability to assist with consistency and humility is how others watch what you do and feed from your energy. People trust consistent actions; they do not trust emotional reactions.

Never allow your service you have been called to whether it is your church, your family, a group of friends, or an organization be questioned because your emotions are leading your service and not your character.

Those who assist out of obligation will never receive the wealth attached to their hands. It should never just benefit you; it should be a blessing to those encountering you and serving with you. When you are serious about your assignment on earth, you begin to allow your influence to infuse those around you.

Servant-leaders are natural innovators. Contrary to what others may think, your youth demands you to be as innovative in your service as possible. Do not be afraid to be wrong in your approach to do right! Because you are still evolving in age and in character, you should begin to master early the ability to deviate from the norm. Allow your natural thought process to shift your serving abilities into gears of excellence and consistency.

For most companies and organizations, they only train you enough to retain you, but not pay you what you are worth. That type of training and coaching only breeds followers and not leaders. Companies and organizations coaching from this perspective generally fear they could be training their replacement or giving too much information to those they have hired. They are afraid employees will take what they have retained and duplicate it somewhere else for their own benefit. If a company fears its employees leaving, it will never develop or produce change agents.

It will never produce people who can successfully carry on the company name, bring new fresh ideas, trust their thoughts, and follow ideas through to completion. Would we like to retain all who we have invested in? Sure, we would! But that is not true growth. True growth is reproduction. It is the planting of an apple seed, the process of germination, and then sprouting out of the ground as an apple tree with "many apples." Growth should mirror the same way.

We sow seeds by training and coaching into one, with the expectation what we have planted in them, they will plant and duplicate in others. Producing more disciples was the intent of Jesus's teaching. He gave his disciples power and authority over all devils to go out and to heal the sick and preach the kingdom of God. (Luke 9:1-2) One of the highlights of this narrative is He gave them power and authority. To some, these words seem similar, however, they serve two purposes.

The word "power" in Greek means dunamis, which refers to "spiritual strength and excellence of soul." Jesus is releasing power to them because of the spiritual forces sent to work against the agenda of God. To combat these forces, the disciples needed power to effectively war in excellence.

Jesus then requires power be paired with authority. Authority (exousia) in its purest definition refers to permission and government. Jesus is simply encouraging his change agents "I not only have given you power and ability, but you also have rights or permission to operate, and to preach with authority and heal with power." I believe this is one of the greatest examples of leadership that is not only productive, but reproductive and transformational.

If we are going to be intentional about growing our churches and organizations, we must begin to transfer power and authority to those under our supervision. We do our servant-leaders an injustice when we only transfer to them tools without direction or words without meaning. We must be intentional about training our replacements.

When I think back to my earlier stages of ministry. I tell everyone I learned to work ministry by observation and transfer. I walked closely enough to those who were functioning in their gifts so everything on the leader, could simply fall on me. When someone did not show up to preside over the worship, I jumped at the opportunity. When someone did not show up to greet guests, I positioned myself in the lobby to do it. When we needed someone to create a program, I got on the computer and began to duplicate what I had seen done while adding my own creative twist. My development in ministry came through "transfer" or what we know to be "on-the-job training."

After school, I made my way to the church, not because I did not have anything else to do or because I was not successful in other arenas. My love for ministry operation and knowledge drew me to where I wanted to be. I wanted to catch the nuggets. I wanted to know more about church polity and church administration. Since they were not offering any classes, I figured the best way to learn was to be around and be engaged.

Those looking to enhance their skills as servant-leaders or in any role of leadership cannot always wait for a class to be offered. This is where you must operate as an autodidact. You must begin to seek the right rooms to obtain the lessons needed to feed your ambition and sharpen your gifts and abilities. Through this type of training came many other lessons made me sensitive to ministry and varying leadership styles. I saw the good, the bad, the mistakes and the intentionality of hurt and love, making me cognizant of people and their perspectives on ministry and leadership.

One of the many benefits of starting young in ministry, especially working closely with leadership, is the art of observation. Observation is a powerful characteristic and in many circles, extremely essential. Servant-leaders should position themselves to observe. Be willing to forfeit your need to pour and substitute it with the need to be a sponge. Much of what we have the ability to learn is often missed in the moment because we fail to shift our posture. You are not weak or unintelligent because you decide to observe instead of speaking. You are wise. I have been afforded the honor to sit in rooms with great men and women of God with substance and sharp minds. My upbringing was simple. Be a sponge instead of a faucet.

Along with the art of observation, there should be a respect for maturation. Young leaders are not dumb, though many are inexperienced. I believe ministry, specifically the local church should be a training ground to prepare, mature and to nurture young servant-leaders. Where there is training there is cultivation. This is the beauty of the local church. Those who are drawn to Her at an early age should be properly nurtured and not used.

Oftentimes we are presented with a one-dimensional perspective of serving in a local assembly because one man or woman, who in most cases the senior leader or visionary, believes everyone under them is inferior. For many years, within the African American Pentecostal and Apostolic tradition, we have, at times, made the local assemblies lesser kingdoms strategically set to serve a personality. That was never the intention or order of the Local Church. The local church was established to render "koinonia"; in other words, "fellowship".

The scripture speaks of this endearing fellowship when it states, *"let us not forsake the assembling of ourselves together, as the manner of some are"* (Hebrews 10:25). If we are not cognizant of anything, I am convinced we should strive to pass on to the next generation of servant-leaders an acute perspective of fellowship! And not fellowship germane to our assigned denomination, organizations, and the like. The coming together of minds and hearts will help foster a greater level of respect and support for the body universally! We place ourselves at a grave disadvantage when we teach our children to be islands unto themselves. Isolation for any leader is never as effective as the company of other consecrated leaders.

For this millennial generation to not repeat the mistakes and mishaps of past leaders, we must be ever committed to education and scholarship. Pay close attention to what your ministry requires pertaining to academics and who you plan to reach with your ministry. I do agree with the premise just as we expect people in other walks of life to be educated and trained, so we should expect those who lead the church.

However, graduation from seminary alone should not be the major qualification for ministry. Spiritual development and spiritual formation are also important. Each denomination and church must establish their own standards. Now, there should be some grace and latitude for those who did not have the benefit of a formal religious education, but who are still qualified in other ways to work their purpose.

We live in a climate filled with influencers and creatives; those who may not have formal credentials or certifications from a four-year university. Yet, they have mastered their crafts to such a degree, they created brands that can serve and teach others. This shift in learning has been impactful in many arenas, especially the church! The church must be willing to employ creatives who are akin to the sons of Issachar (1 Chr. 12:32), who are well-versed in the discernment of the times and have the creative genius to implement policies, procedures and infrastructures that will assist local assemblies in healthy transitions and growth.

The Apostle Paul is a great example of this idea and thought. With all his ability he was in many cases challenged by those churches he was assigned to contribute to and serve. In second Corinthians 10:1-11, Paul responded to the bold accusations his presence and rhetoric failed to compliment his writings to the church at Corinth. Paul steadily defended his apostolicism compared to those false apostles who invaded Corinth after his departure. Paul's challenge with the Corinthians is relevant even in today's hour. Corinth was a port city with vast economic gain which made them arrogant and effortlessly persuaded by false teachings. This made their giving of gifts and resources a strain, but Paul was equipped; not just because of formal training but through empirical transformation.

We know Paul's experience differed from the other 12 apostles as recorded in scripture. He did not consult man as it pertained to his gospel teaching but consulted Jesus Christ directly. Paul had early formal teaching through a Jewish upbringing and then is established further. He considered himself to be a Hebrew of Hebrews, a Pharisee and disciple of Gamaliel (Phil. 3:5). Paul was well versed in scripture. He understood Aramaic and penned his letters in Greek. But Paul's greatest training and influence was established by his embrace and understanding of world and culture.

This was useful in Paul's establishments of the Macedonia Church who were not as wealthy as the Corinthians but graced by God to experience unspeakable joy (2 Cor 8:1-2) This abundance of joy served as the catalyst for their faith and generosity. Paul's diverse approach to ministry and culture, along with his strength to self-educate, made his pastoral and administrative reach effective even when not appreciated.

Paul's efficacy was a result of his knowledge and aptitude to cite scholars and thinkers of his day who embraced other theologies and schools of thought. While perhaps an affront to the religious scholars of the time, it was necessary for Paul's development.

You must be willing to go against the grain to remain effective and in some cases, relevant. The year 2020 will go down in history as the year that gave validity to the creativity and innovation of the millennial! The church would not have survived without a millennial on staff. Companies, organizations, and even schools would not have continued without properly employing the right creative minds with the wit and fearlessness to refashion and create new infrastructure. This creativity assisted these organizations to continue being able to serve their communities. That is servant-leadership personified. It is possessing the bandwidth to adjust and not be overwhelmed by controversy and conflict.

I can recall an opportunity afforded to me to preach at a certain church for a very well-respected pastor. It appeared the invitation came out of nowhere. However, this particular pastor's young adults heard me in a worship service they had attended. They shared their experience with the life changing word the Lord had allowed me to deliver. They expressed an appreciation for my authenticity and sincere ministry. Because of their recommendation, their pastor was led to invite me to his church for his church's anniversary. This was a great opportunity.

I had never been so nervous in my entire life. My anxiety was a result of my reverence for the invitation and the pastor who had extended it. After sending the invite to my pastor, (protocol taught us to be released before accepting invites) he allowed me to accept. I was excited but did not share it with anyone at the time. A few days passed. I felt released to share the invite with a preacher friend of mine. In ministry, I have not had many friends. As I finished sharing the news, he responded reluctantly and from a place of disbelief. He proceeded to ask, "Are you sure they sent it to you? Are you sure it was not for Bishop?"

Appalled and somewhat confused, I showed him the invitation and he responded, "Cool." After I dropped him off, I began to question my calling and my abilities. I could not address my so-called friend because their perception of me no longer held any significance.

However, in that moment, I began to unknowingly compare myself to my father/pastor, which was so unwise. This was not because I wanted to be him but what I had heard my entire life-- you sound like him, you preach like him, you stand like him. As flattering and as humbling those comments were, this particular invitation was a defining moment for me. It highlighted a truth that could not be denied. My authenticity, my ministry had been sought out and it was not because of my last name.

In this season of definition, do not become so immersed by how others choose to define you, you fail to prepare for your defining moment. A defining moment is a point, in your life, when you are urged to make a pivotal decision or when you experience something that fundamentally changes you. Not only do these moments define us; they have an effect on our perceptions and behaviors. This has been a lifelong lesson and continues to be a place of perfection for me.

When you are leading and blazing trails in any capacity, you will be forced into the arena of comparison. It is almost impossible to escape considering the climate in which we exist and how addicted to social media algorithms we have become. If you are not careful, you will be trying to keep up with fads that are fading and attempting to prove points to people whose opinions are not worth your energy. Any way you look at it, I want you to leave comparison where it belongs - in the column of irrelevancy.

Do not allow comparison to weaken your commitment to your calling! You are enough. God has equipped you with everything you need to flow and produce quality fruit even at a young age.

JUSTIN MARSHALL

Justin Spencer Marshall was born the second son of Bishop Freddie Marshall and Lady Sheri Bratcher on October 29th, 1991. He is a native of the triad area, Winston-Salem, North, Carolina. He received his education through the Forsyth County School System. Pastor Marshall was raised in a Christian home with a Pentecostal upbringing. Being a faithful member of his home church, Christ Cathedral of the Triad, he has been taught the importance of serving the local church and being a faithful follower of leadership and committed disciple of Jesus Christ.

Licensed to preach in the year 2009, Pastor Marshall has served not just his home church but the body of Christ at large. He currently serves faithfully and vigorously as the Executive Assistant Pastor of his home church and his ministry prowess include, leadership training and development for auxiliary leaders and para-church leaders.

Pastor Marshall believes in servant-leadership and encourages ministry gifts through his preaching and teaching as well as his newly released book entitled "Ministry Matters: A Guide for the Millennial Servant-Leader", to embrace the blueprint for kingdom greatness Jesus released to his disciples in Matthew 20, *"but whosoever will be great among you, let him be your minister; and whosoever will be chief among you, let him be your servant"*

He is married to the beautiful Alicia Mone't Marshall and they have one son, Ethan Spencer Marshall. He and his wife believe in the holistic perspective of growth including God, Family, and Ministry!

REFLECTION

Young But Not Dumb

"You need friends that have grace for your growth."

I started my church at 21 years old. Just like with starting any other profession, there was a lot I did not know but I had an old soul. I was acquainted with church all my life and sat with many church fathers. I was able to glean what I like to call "the other stuff". You know, those things no university or seminary could teach.

Because of my age, I was many times mistaken as someone with all zeal and no skill. This was sad because I needed to learn from the Fathers of my city. Many were closed completely to helping "this young buck" and some were even quite arrogant. Then there were those who wanted to help me, but their attitude was condescending. I wanted mentorship, but I was smart enough to know mentorship requires humility on both parts. You can show a person the way without making them feel unintelligent or "dumb"

Because I felt outnumbered and misunderstood, I asked God to send true friends. He did. True friends get who you are. They have the capacity to handle the weight of your assignment. Youthfulness is in no way synonymous with ignorant. It simply means you have to grow into your assignment. A wise man once said, "Only two professions start at the top. That's well digging and grave digging. Everything else, you have to work yourself up."

Remove yourself from every relationship that makes you feel comfortable being who you were never supposed to be. You cannot fight the devil and the negativity of false help. When you remove yourself from who you don't need to be connected to, you open the door for right connections.

- If they do not know you personally, do not take it personally. Do not let social media cause you to lose every bit of influence and credibility you have. Think twice before posting.

18

Serving Made Easy

Elder Myron Jones
Executive Assistant to the
General Overseer of Armorbearers |
Full Gospel Baptist Church Fellowship
Atlanta, GA

My mom had me when she was 20 years of age. My primary years were spent with my grandmother in Alabama. At two years of age, I contracted spinal meningitis. I was hospitalized for two months and my grandmother stayed every day with me. God had His hand on me even before I totally understood. After being released from the hospital, the left side of my body was affected. I walked with a limp. I am deaf in my left ear, and occasionally I will talk to one side of my face. The limp is gone, and I know God is still able to give me a full restoration. Eventually, my mom and my stepfather wanted me at home with them. So, I left my grandmother in Alabama and moved to Atlanta with my parents in 1986.

Growing up in a God-fearing family, salvation was taught for as long as I can remember. Salvation was taken to a more intimate level once I moved home with my mom. I accepted Christ as my Lord and Savior in 1987 when I was 8 years of age. My family church, in Atlanta is Christ Christian Church. Anthony Larry Long Sr. is Pastor. Under his teachings and God's direction, I grew closer to God. I desired to please God. I wanted God to live and dwell in me. And in 1988, His dwelling in me became prevalent through speaking in tongues .

I have been a servant all of my life. I grew up in the house with my mother and stepfather. It was necessary for me to be the stepchild, so God could further solidify my understanding of being grafted in. It is in Romans 11:17 where Paul uses the analogy of an olive branch. Farmers would break off dead branches and attach live branches. They wrapped the branch to the tree until it become attached. Paul was encouraging the Gentiles not to get arrogant because they chose Jesus, and the Jews did not. However, if Jesus gave us, Gentiles, a chance how much more will He do for the Jews.

Being in a nondenominational church birthed out of the Pentecostal movement, was rough for me as a child. Even as children we fasted, had to attend service 3 times a week, evangelize on the weekends and feed the homeless regularly. All I knew was how to serve God, His people, and my leader. It started with being an usher and grew to be more due to my availability and commitment. I definitely was not the most capable or anointed at the time, but because of my willingness to be used, He graced me with His favor and anointing.

My stepfather had three children before he married my mother. My mother had me. Together, they had six. So, at any given time there could have been ten of us in the house. However, the blessing of this for me was God allowed me to see and feel the grafting in by my stepfather. From the view of the world, Carlos Juan Mosley Sr. was my stepfather. To me he was my Daddy. He taught me hard work pays off. He reminded me the way to the top was being available and ready with a humble spirit. He would tell me no work beneath me. He and my mother consistently reminded me recognition does not come from your people, it comes from the quality of your presentation and your availability.

This thought process thrust me into becoming a key servant of my church. I would serve when my pastor would minister/prophecy to the people. That was huge for me. You could not usher with the prophet unless they believed you were full of the Holy Ghost and had the spirit of discernment. So, I was overjoyed when I was considered! However, this was the beginning of the process of "Serving Made Easy!"

To truly understand how to serve you must first know who you work for. Is work a place of drudgery and pain? Or is work a place of reverence and devotion? I have come to understand that work is a crude form of worship. When we reverence our serving, relationships, jobs, and all of our involvements as we do God then and only then do we begin to walk in the fullness of God. Colossians 3:23-24 tells us *23 Whatever you do, work at it with all your heart, as working for the Lord, not for human masters, 24 since you know that you will receive an inheritance from the Lord as a reward. It is the Lord Christ you are serving.*

I worked hard trying to please man. I wanted men to validate me by accepting me. I did not need their verbal accolades however, I wanted to be liked and validated by their acceptance. I realized this was a deep-seated issue I had dealt with even in my matriculation as a middle and high school student. I just wanted to be accepted. I began to judge God by how He allowed me to be accepted by others. This was a trick of the enemy to take my faith. we know the Word of God tells us in Hebrews 11:6: *"But without faith it is impossible to please him: for he that cometh to God must believe that He is, and that he is a rewarder of them that diligently seek Him."*

It seemed to me every leader I had, believed I wasn't good enough. I was consistently corrected and very seldomly validated. The validation I desired was never with their lip service but by their action. I wanted relationship/sonship. I wanted to reverence them because of the relationship, not out of fear of correction. I desired to be honest and not be judged. I looked in the mirror, saw the lack of validation was real and the hurt was unbearable simply because of my perspective of self.

I had to come to understand that you cannot have faith without the right perspective. Faith is a muscle. The more we practice our faith, the stronger the muscle becomes. So, in order for an individual to make a lifestyle change, the change must happen in their perspective. The practicing of our faith must begin with the change of our perspective. I had to realize I did not see myself as a servant of God but as a servant to my leader. Even though I did not want verbal praise or recognition; the relationship I desired, in itself was still a false sense of praise. I had to come to understand if I seek God for relationship and serve as unto him, He will send me a leader who would mentor me and allow me to have sonship. This sonship was not a façade, but God given, and it has fulfilled me.

Ultimately, I came to realization of who I work for. I don't work for man but for GOD! Ephesians 6:5-8 states *"Servants, respectfully obey your earthly masters but always with an eye to obeying the real master, Christ. Don't just do what you have to do to get by, but work heartily, as Christ's servants doing what God wants you to do. And work with a smile on your face, always keeping in mind that 'No' matter who happens to be giving the orders, you're really serving God. Good work will get you good pay from the Master, regardless of whether you are slave or free."* I desired what only God can give. I wanted it from man. This thought process caused me a whole lot of heartache, but God is faithful.

In 2017, God allowed my wife and I to get employment in Dubai. We taught English, Math & Science to students in the Middle East. I thought this was going to be one of the best financial moves I could ever make for my family. However, I was still trying to find validation and since I did not feel I was getting it from my leader, I was going to travel. I was going to become more financially stable with the idea "then they will see I am somebody". God allowed me to go but the lesson I learned was greater than I could have ever imagined.

While in the Middle East, God showed me first-hand what Jesus said in Matthew 22:37-39 *"37Jesus said unto him, Thou shalt love the Lord thy God with all thy heart, and with all thy soul, and with all thy mind. 38 This is the first and great commandment. 39 And the second is like unto it, Thou shalt love thy neighbor as thyself."* My perspective became even clearer. I must love how God loves! In the Middle East there are churches and mosques on the same street. Christians and Muslims respected the sacred times of each other's worship.

When the Islamic time of Ramadan came, I assisted other Christians preparing food so when the sun set, Muslims would have food to eat. God allowed me to travel to the other side of the world to truly learn of Him so my perspective could become clearer. I work for God and He elevates and promotes! Matthew 23:11 says *"The greatest among you will be your servant."* I had the serving down, but my perspective was all wrong. Serving made easy became a reality when I finally understood who I work for.

MYRON JONES

Myron David Jones, Sr. was born in Demopolis, Alabama but raised in South Fulton County GA. He grew up in a blended family with his nine siblings and parents Carlos & Diane Mosley. He attended Georgia Southern University in Statesboro, GA. where he met his beautiful wife Shandra. Through his love for family, young people, and education he went back to school and received his bachelors' and master's degrees in Early Childhood Education and Special Education from Mercer University.

Elder Jones served as the State Director of Armorbearers for Georgia in the Full Gospel Baptist Church Fellowship for a number of years. Currently Elder Jones is the Regional Director of Armorbearers of the Southern Atlantic Region and he is the Executive Assistant to the General Overseer of Armorbearers in the Full Gospel Baptist Church Fellowship.

Elder Jones and the love of his life, Shandra, have been married for 16 years. They have three beautiful children, Naomi Grace, Leah Gabrielle, and Myron Jr. Elder Jones has a passion for serving and being a blessing to God's people. As an Elder at THE RHEMANATION CHURCH, under the leadership of Pastor Vanessa Hall, he serves as Director of the IGNITE ministry and Director of The Rhema Nation Community Foundation. Elder Jones declares, "I love God and I count it an honor and a privilege to serve."

REFLECTION

Serving Made Easy
"I want to be around people who still think it is
cool to help others grow."

In Charles Dicken's Doctor Marigold, he writes, "No one is useless in this world who lightens the burdens of another." When you are called to serve others, it becomes as natural a breathing. You want to see people grow and become the best they can be at everything. We are living in a time, where there is so much competition and comparison, it can be difficult at times to find persons who are not tied to their own self-aggrandizement.

Sometimes to see people reach their potential, you have to release them to others, for a period, who can teach them things you cannot. Every leader needs to know two things; when to release and when to empower. If the truth be known, most of us have failed at both. I served leaders who empowered me to go beyond the limitations of the church and step into the unlimited possibilities of the Kingdom. I observed leaders who restricted and constrained those who served them because of their fear of being diminished. I received the accolades of one who recognized and released spiritual sons and daughters to flow in their God-given anointing. And, I have been accused of not adequately "honoring" or properly "acknowledging" those who served my ministry. Either way, I had to manage both the honor of the success and the weight of the failure.

It is always my personal commitment to help others become all God intended for them to be if they choose to. But, that can only be accomplished through relationships, rooted in our ability to serve one another. In this season, it is my desire to be to others what I have needed the most.

• Genuine relationship is the connection of the heart, not the creation of opportunities.

A Final Word

It is so easy to watch people serve in ministry and be enamored by the highlights, without a clue of the depth of their story. When you watch the highlight reel of a football game on the 11:00 o'clock news, you only see edited segments of the games. You see major moves, big plays, turnovers, and ultimately the final score. You don't see the preparation for the game; the full duration of the game; every blow, every penalty; or each individual comment from the crowd. All you get to see are edited moments where the player is spotlighted. The game entails much more than the moments you were afforded to watch. There are so many awesome people around this country, too many to name, who work behind the scenes and make ministry happen for their leaders. They are indeed the "hidden figures" who I want to celebrate.

In the late 90's I had the opportunity to go to the Bahamas and share in a conference hosted by the late Myles Munroe. Once I concluded my presentation, he said to the people, "This man is a King-Maker". At the time, I was a young pastor with little to offer anybody; but I knew someday I would be presented with opportunities not necessarily for me, but rather for others. As part of my assignment in life, I am anointed to point. I point to others who are doing things I could never or would never do. I am called upon as a servant leader by many in the Body of Christ, but the movers and shakers in the kingdom are those who may never have their names called. To be a servant leader cost. Each person pays differently which makes our collective stories a tapestry of interdependence. I compiled this book to say, Your life matters. Your service matters. You matter.

I hope, from these stories and experiences, you have gained some insight, knowledge, and wisdom as you continue to serve in the Kingdom of God. Each of these servant leaders has had to grapple with the age-old question, "Is my service really appreciated by those I give myself for?" True servanthood is never an event, but it is a journey. These brothers and sisters have endured the warfare, the wilderness, the wrong accusations, and the weight that accompanies being a servant leader. These few pages cannot fully describe for you what a commitment to service has cost them.

Each of them I know personally. These are beautiful relationships established over time. I have been privileged to celebrate their amazing accomplishments and to weep with them when the weight seemed too much to bear. I know they are committed servants, men and women of God who have had amazing triumphs; defied insurmountable odds; and beat overwhelming obstacles. They have made the decision serving is the only way to go. They serve not to live but they live to serve. Serving is their life. If I know nothing else, I know this. All of us are finding our place, doing our part, and fulfilling our purpose, while we serve.

About the Author

Bishop Randy Borders, an anointed preacher of our time, communicates the gospel message with unmistakable clarity. His ministry challenges believers to flow in God's Divine Order.

He is a graduate of The University of North Carolina at Greensboro.
in 1990, Bishop Borders founded Word of Life Fellowship Church. The church name was officially changed to Faith Harvest Church in March of 1999. Bishop Borders currently serves as senior pastor of Faith Harvest Church, in Shelby, NC.

Faith Harvest Church has evolved into a multiracial, multifaceted ministry, which include many ministries of edification and outreach. Bishop Borders is also Founder and Presiding Prelate of Harvest Ministries International, Inc., a network of local churches with primary vision of church planting and strengthening. Since his consecration, Bishop Borders has become part of the Joint College of African American Pentecostal Bishops Congress, where he serves as a member of the Executive Board. He also serves as the Bishop of Armorbearers for the Full Gospel Baptist Church Fellowship.

In June of 2002, Bishop Borders founded Christ Harvest Church in Charlotte, NC. He also founded Covenant Harvest Church in Greer, SC in November of 2009.

Bishop Borders met the former Norma Lee while attending UNCG. The two were married in June 1994, and have two lovely children-Efrim and Hope.

A published author of the critically acclaimed books STAY FOCUSED, THE ADJUTANT'S GUIDE TO ETIQUETTE, MORE THAN A MENTOR and now STORIES FROM SERVANT LEADERS. Bishop Borders travels extensively throughout the United States and abroad as a lecturer, conference speaker, revivalist, and seminar speaker.

The ministry of Bishop Borders is bold, energetic, and dynamic- equipping the saints to lock into their pastor's vision and fulfill their destiny. Many who have experienced his ministry have this testimony Bishop Borders is definitely a pastor's friend.